PRAISE FOR *OVER IT*

"Lolo is a special athlete. To compete in multiple Olympics—especially in two different sports—requires incredible talent and drive. More importantly, the way Lolo has faced challenges and persevered through hardships should be an inspiration to all."

—MICHAEL PHELPS, TWENTY-THREE-TIME OLYMPIC GOLD MEDALIST

"Lolo is a champion. Champions don't experience triumph without trial. Her pain and purpose will inspire us all."

—LECRAE, GRAMMY-WINNING ARTIST AND
NEW YORK TIMES BESTSELLING AUTHOR

"Lolo Jones's book *Over It* is truly inspiring and thought provoking. Imagine being in a stadium of 100,000 people and yards away from Olympic gold. It is a point that most people could only dream of and Lolo was there. Then imagine handling the outcome either way it goes from there. What Lolo shares in this book in detail is a life lesson for all of us. It's a book everyone should read."

—NICK NURSE, HEAD COACH OF THE 2019 WORLD CHAMPIONS,
2020 NBA COACH OF THE YEAR, AND A FELLOW IOWAN

"So much can be learned from life's struggles. This book provides myriad examples of how Lolo's determination, grit, and unwavering belief in herself enabled her to overcome innumerable roadblocks and hardships."

—DENNIS SHAVER, LSU TRACK AND FIELD HEAD COACH

"The best advice I've ever received is 'Do your best and let God handle the rest.' This life view is simple yet powerful. Do the best with what you have direct control over, prepare, and be ready when opportunity presents itself. Lolo's life shines this message brightly for the entire world to see.

Lolo has worked hard her entire life and overcome obstacles that would have broken most people. Yet she has consistently demonstrated resilience and perseverance that are truly incredible. She has been humble in her successes and gracious in her failures. There is no quitting in her. She is a true role model.

To all the young girls out there: no one is coming to rescue you, no one is coming to give you your dreams, *you* have to take your life and your destiny into your own hands. Don't be afraid of hard work, it builds discipline. Don't be afraid of failure, it builds perseverance. Don't be afraid of rejection, it breeds resilience. Success is where preparation and opportunity meet, so make sure you are the best prepared person in any room. Align yourself with people who are motivated and positive and who can help you become a better version of yourself. You are worthy of success. You are worthy of achieving your dreams. So follow Lolo's example and start working toward them!"

—Natalie Eva Marie, professional athlete, actress, and WWE Superstar

"Anyone who knows or has followed Lolo has witnessed how incredibly strong she is—physically, of course, but also mentally and spiritually. She's experienced things in her life that would crush most people, yet she kept pushing through to become the best of the best in two sports! Lolo's openness and vulnerability in her new book shows a side of her that most people haven't seen yet. *Over It* is going to help so many people who are experiencing or have experienced similar hard times realize that things can and will get better if they just work at it. Lolo's story is proof that there is a light at the end of the tunnel, that there is a purpose in the pain, and that anyone can come out on top."

—Katrín Davíðsdóttir, two-time Fittest Woman on Earth

"Professional sports can be an incredibly cruel environment, mentally and physically, and the best athletes are those who are able to manage both the internal and external pressures. Lolo is someone I got to know a couple years ago, and I realized immediately that her athletic capability is just one example of the incredible strength she possesses. What she has experienced throughout her career and personal life is enough to derail even the best of us, but her indelible faith and fighting spirit have pushed her to heights that most can only dream of. Her story is one of perseverance, honesty, and beauty as she allows us to come along on her journey, proving that the road less traveled is often full of obstacles but can be immensely rewarding if we are willing to take the first step."

—ALEXANDER ROSSI, INDYCAR DRIVER

"As a professional athlete myself, reading about Lolo Jones's story is nothing short of inspirational. She's overcome so many odds and adversities in her life that they are a testament to her unrelenting passion for sports. Very few can say that at one point in time, they were one of the best hurdlers in the world. Lolo Jones is one of them. She took her passion and heartbreak from one sport and threw it into another (bobsledding), and she rebuilt herself to win another world championship in a completely different sport. Lolo Jones is proof that it is never too late to fight for your dreams. Her story is a must-read for anyone who wants to be inspired."

—NATTIE NEIDHART, WWE SUPERSTAR

"Lolo has an unwavering commitment to achieve her goals. She competes with an indomitable will in Olympic competitions where the margin for error is unforgiving and mercilessly thin. Lolo is a fierce competitor and one of the most tenacious athletes I have ever worked with in bobsled."

—MIKE KOHN, USA BOBSLED HEAD COACH

"Lolo is the hardest-working training partner I've had in my career as a professional. She's constantly in pursuit of perfection, and as result, she is her own biggest critic. This approach has allowed her to overcome obstacles unimaginable to many on the outside, but not to those who see her daily grind."

—RICHARD THOMPSON, THREE-TIME OLYMPIC MEDALIST

"I've had the privilege to know some great athletes. But it is exhilarating to know the special ones. Lolo Jones owns the rare distinction of being *both* a Summer and a Winter Olympian, never mind a world champion. Punctuate these accomplishments with her charm, beauty, and technicolor personality, and you have a book you must read."

—GENE MCCARTHY, FORMER PRESIDENT AND CEO, ASICS AMERICA

"As a Mr. Olympia, I've always known Lolo for her toughness in the gym and as a champion athlete. But this book has taught me so much more about her mental toughness and how much she had to overcome to get to the Olympics in the first place. Her grit, determination, and faith can serve as an inspiration to anyone who is going through a tough time and needs a light to help guide them."

—FLEX LEWIS, SEVEN-TIME MR. OLYMPIA

OVER IT

OVER IT

How to Face Life's Hurdles with
Grit, Hustle, and Grace

LOLO JONES

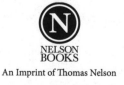

NELSON
BOOKS

An Imprint of Thomas Nelson

Published in Nashville, Tennessee, by Nelson Books, an imprint of Thomas Nelson. Nelson Books and Thomas Nelson are registered trademarks of HarperCollins Christian Publishing, Inc.

Author is represented by The Fedd Agency, Inc., P. O. Box 341973, Austin, Texas 78734.

Thomas Nelson titles may be purchased in bulk for educational, business, fundraising, or sales promotional use. For information, please e-mail SpecialMarkets@ ThomasNelson.com.

Unless otherwise noted, Scripture quotations taken from The Holy Bible, New International Version®, NIV®. Copyright © 1973, 1978, 1984, 2011 by Biblica, Inc.® Used by permission of Zondervan. All rights reserved worldwide. www.Zondervan.com. The "NIV" and "New International Version" are trademarks registered in the United States Patent and Trademark Office by Biblica, Inc.®

Scripture quotations marked ESV are taken from the ESV® Bible (The Holy Bible, English Standard Version®). Copyright © 2001 by Crossway, a publishing ministry of Good News Publishers. Used by permission. All rights reserved.

Scripture quotations marked KJV are taken from the King James Version. Public domain.

Any internet addresses, phone numbers, or company or product information printed in this book are offered as a resource and are not intended in any way to be or to imply an endorsement by Thomas Nelson, nor does Thomas Nelson vouch for the existence, content, or services of these sites, phone numbers, companies, or products beyond the life of this book.

ISBN: 978-1-4002-2419-7 (HC)
ISBN: 978-1-4002-2420-3 (ePub)
ISBN: 978-1-4002-2422-7 (Audiobook)

Library of Congress Control Number: 2021933068

Printed in the United States of America

21 22 23 24 25   LSC   10 9 8 7 6 5 4 3 2 1

To all those who wanted to quit but took one more step.

Success consists of going from failure to failure without loss of enthusiasm.

—Winston Churchill

CONTENTS

ONE

BUT YOU'RE HERE

It was 2008. I was warming up on a track outside the nest-like structure of the Beijing National Stadium with two hundred other Olympic athletes and coaches. There were a lot of cameras, but I barely noticed them. I was focused.

My coach's words, "Just do what you did to get here," were instructing my subconscious as I tuned out any possible distractions, including the unfamiliar outside pressure of being expected to win.

On the plane ride over to Beijing, I had sat next to a man who was reading *USA Today*. I'd tried not to look, but I couldn't help myself. On the turned-out page the headline read "Lolo Jones Expected to Win Gold."

Over the last month I'd heard it all. "She's gonna break the world record." "She's on pace to break the Olympic record." And I was.

No one had known my name eleven months earlier, but I'd had the season of my life, winning most of my races, breaking records, and making my first Olympic team along the way.

There had been a huge buildup to this day. But now I was tuning all that out; I was focused. And I was confident.

Not overly so, but I was ready to execute, and I knew it.

I'd run a smooth, easy race in the Olympic prelims. And yesterday's semifinals had been the best race of my life, even though I'd actually slowed at the end so I could conserve energy for today's final. Plus, there were no aches or pains. My body was in the best shape it had ever been.

Just a couple of hours ago, I'd gone to the first call room, a very small room filled with Olympic officials and my competitors, the seven girls I was going to compete against for an Olympic medal. The officials confirmed our lanes, checked our spikes and our bib numbers, and inspected our uniforms to confirm that everything was sanctioned.

I'd felt everybody's nerves. Legs shaking. Girls visualizing and breathing heavily, talking to themselves.

Then we were led to a larger call room underneath the stadium. This room had a small track, a sprint area where we could stay warmed up or work out our nerves while we waited. We could hear the muffled roar of people cheering their country's athletes in the elite competitions taking place just outside. This was the Olympics.

I was at the Games, but it was just another race for me. Then . . .

The officials walked us out into the Olympic Stadium.

More than a hundred thousand people were cheering in the stands, and I could feel my nerves trying to overpower me. I took a deep breath.

I was calm in the eye of a storm. I knew there was a crowd, along with the lights and cameras, and I was aware of the expectations. But I blocked it all out. I actually felt peaceful.

Let everything swirl around me. Let them go crazy. Let them take their pictures. *Let them be loud. Let them wave their countries' flags while they cheer the long jumper, the pole vaulter, the sprinter, the hurdler. I am in the eye of the storm. I am focused on what I am going to do,* I thought.

I took a deep breath. *Just do what you did to get here,* I instructed my subconscious as I took my warm-ups off and got set in my blocks for a practice start. I was so mentally strong in that moment that I couldn't even hear my own mother who was cheering at the top of her lungs.

Five minutes before the gun, the nerves can get you.

There have been races where I wasn't confident, and in those five minutes I'd find myself looking at the girl next to me and thinking, *That girl looks incredible.* But none of that was happening at the Beijing final. In those seconds before the race, I couldn't have told you who was running in each lane, or even who was next to me.

Nothing distracted me. With my hands I visualized my position, how my body would be in the blocks. I visualized my first few steps. I focused on my approach to the first hurdle, on the momentum I would gain in that moment.

The starter yelled, "Runners, take your mark."

I approached the line, shook my legs, and got into the blocks.

"Set."

The gun went off.

The Australian girl got out on me.

I didn't panic; we had raced a lot over the course of the season. I knew she would have a great start, but I also knew I would be able to catch her by hurdle three.

I did.

I passed her, and from hurdles three through five, I was in an amazing rhythm and knew I was winning the race.

I wasn't thinking, *I'm winning the Olympic gold medal.* It just felt like another race. But I was executing at the highest level.

And then there was a point after hurdle five when I thought, *Wow, these hurdles are coming up really, really fast.*

In that moment my body was running the fastest it had ever run. To adjust for the speed, I focused on turnover to make my steps quicker between the hurdles. I knew I couldn't get sloppy with my technique, so I told myself to make sure my legs were snapping out.

But I turned over too much between the hurdles, and instead of relaxing I overcompensated. It was a small miscalculation with an epic ramification. Hurdles are only ten meters apart. Your steps between them must be perfect. As I approach a hurdle, if my big toe is over my takeoff point by even half an inch, that can mess up all of my angles.

I should have relaxed a little bit and just run. Instead, I was so paranoid because the hurdles were coming so fast that I snapped my lead foot down too quickly. Then I caught the ninth hurdle and rode it to the ground. I was finally able to get my foot off the hurdle, and thought I would still be able to get a medal. But as I crossed the line and looked up at the board, I saw I got seventh.

Seventh.

I collapsed on the track, and I couldn't stop thinking, *I just wish the next Olympics were tomorrow.* I was heartbroken as my mind tried to understand what I'd lost.[1]

Then, in front of millions watching around the globe, on my knees, fighting tears, feeling the crushing immediate weight of disappointment, I sensed God whispering to me, *But you're here.*

That thought was followed by a memory from four years earlier. I remembered how I watched the Athens 2004 Olympic Games from my Baton Rouge, Louisiana, apartment; how I cried because I hadn't made that Olympic team, because I was watching others do what I knew I could do, because I knew I was born to compete with the best in the world at an Olympic Games.

Now, on an Olympic track in Beijing, I sensed God saying, *But you're here.*

Those three words flooded my heart with a sense of thankfulness and peace. Maybe the kind of peace written about in Philippians 4:7, the peace that "surpasses all understanding" (ESV).

It didn't erase the pain, the crushing blow of a loss, but it gave me another perspective. A higher and more hopeful perspective.

But you're here.

There was a lifetime of truth in those three words.

God spoke to my heart at the moment of my greatest professional disappointment and gave me a means, even in tears, even in pain, to move forward.

Those words provided solid ground upon which I could stand. From those words I could access peace, gratitude, a sense of accomplishment, joy, hope, on and on . . .

But you're here. I could write a book based on those three words.

OVER IT

The idea of getting over hurdles is used so often by people who are facing adversity while pursuing their dreams that the book title *Over It* could come across as cliché.

But it's not a cliché to me.

For me, "over it" is about working out six hours a day, six days a week, running until I puke, and then running some more. "Over it" is about lifting weights until every muscle is screaming, then lifting more.

"Over it" is about risking the possibility of hitting a hurdle that could literally end my career.

When I hit that penultimate hurdle in the 2008 Games, I felt like the whole world was watching me lose, seeing my dreams go down with me.

There are ten hurdles in the 100 meter. I was winning the race when I hit the ninth.

So close, and yet so agonizingly far.

In 2008, before the Games, I won my first world championship. By the time I got to Beijing I was winning almost every race. I was athletically peaking, favored to win, and, before hitting that hurdle, on pace for a possible Olympic record. I was nine-tenths of the way to likely achieving a gold medal when tragedy struck. Or more accurately, when I struck tragedy.

I didn't just lose a race; I lost a race I was clearly winning.

I went from first to seventh in the blink of an eye.

Me on my knees beating the track in disbelieving heartbreak has pretty much become an iconic Olympic image. That loss resonates with people. I know, because it's brought up often. I think it's because everyone has experienced the pain of failure, loss, and disappointment. The outcome of that race was vividly and uncomplicatedly true, and any viewer with a shred of empathy felt it.

As an Olympic hurdler who has dedicated my life to perfecting the 100-meter hurdle, I can assure you that the sport is greatly nuanced, but for the casual viewer, a hurdles race can appear pretty straightforward. Eight competitors line up, a gun sounds, and they burst from the blocks, each with the same goal: to overcome ten hurdles in the span of 100 meters and reach the finish line faster than the other seven girls.

In a hurdles race, success and failure are clearly defined by how an individual hurdler performs. Unlike team sports, winning and losing are singularly determined. If you lose, there is no poor call by the ref that you can blame, no teammates to throw under the bus. The

100-meter hurdles are just made up of eight self-motivated, highly focused women seeking to achieve 12-second perfection.

Twelve seconds. That is approximately how long it takes to run an Olympic hurdles race. And when I write *approximately*, it's because the race is won in the last hundredth of that twelfth second.

And that's why, for me, the metaphor of hurdling is a perfect way to describe my life.

Over the course of twenty years, I have sought to achieve perfection in a race that lasts only 12 seconds. I have learned that to achieve success I have to be intensely self-motivated and singularly focused. I have to be willing to risk falling; to get scars on my legs, hips, arms, and shoulders; to rip hamstrings, rupture ankles, fracture bones, and cry myself to sleep at night because of the pain. And all along the way I have had to overcome the emotional and relational disappointments that try to knock me off track.

So, "over it" is way more than a cliché to me. You see, I have given my life to make it true.

Do you know the odds of making it into an Olympics? For swimmers, it's 0.0013 percent.[2] And as a hurdler, I did it twice!

Actually, if you count the Winter Games, and everybody does, then the number of Olympics I've competed in is three. Something I know only ten other Americans have done in the history of the Olympics.

There are almost eight billion people in the world, and only three US hurdlers can compete in any one Olympic Games. So I could say, "I beat the odds . . . three times."

Attack, attack, attack. Keep going. Don't quit. Work harder than everyone around you. Then work even harder, believe in yourself, forgive yourself, forgive those who hurt you along the way, practice gratitude, trust God, trust God, trust God.

Did I mention don't quit?

I have had my share of hurdles, literally and in life. I know a thing or two about how to clear a hurdle to achieve your goals, to experience success.

I'm all about goals achieved, and I hope this book both inspires and helps you clear your own hurdles as you push toward your personal goals. But I've learned that achieving a goal and experiencing success are not always the same thing. Success isn't always defined by a goal achieved. It is truly defined by how we handle failure and disappointment while pursuing our goals.

Some of the most amazing, successful moments in my life have been the most painful, those times I didn't cleanly clear the hurdle. I think success in life is often discovered after you have given everything you have to achieve a goal, only to hit the ninth hurdle and come up short.

HEALTHY HINDSIGHT

It's a fascinating thing about us humans. We often remember the losses and disappointments better than our successes and breakthroughs. For me, 2008 is like that. My traumatic loss is more memorable than any of my traditional wins. When people think about Lolo Jones the hurdler, most don't recall my American record and world championship gold medals, or how I became the first female hurdler to defend a world championship title. But that loss . . . it's remembered.

Thirteen years later, there is rarely an interview in which I am not asked about it. And that's fine; I don't mind talking about it. It's a part of my story.

I have become practiced at deflecting any pain by giving

lighthearted and humorous answers. In fact, I did another interview recently where we discussed 2008.

"In hindsight, if you had a cheat sheet, what would you tell your younger self?" the interviewer asked.

"I would probably tell myself not to hit the ninth hurdle that cost me a gold medal," I answered, laughing.[3]

But in this book, I'm pulling back the curtain.

The fact is, that memory has become more painful as the years pass because of the stacking disappointments since.

To this day, I have never discussed 2008 with my coach. We always break down the races, the wins, and especially the losses. But not that one. Thirteen years have gone by, and we still don't talk about it. There have been no discussions around why or how I hit that ninth hurdle, no conversations about what happened after.

I've told myself it's too painful for my coach, that he doesn't want to talk about it. And maybe that's true. But I think we both know that it's too painful for me.

I think we can all look back at something in our lives that we would have done differently, a painful moment or disappointment we would change. We all wonder, *If I had a cheat sheet, what would be different today?*

But hindsight isn't about changing our past; it's about using our past to form our future.

I hit that hurdle; I can't change that, and it hurts. But I have used that experience, and even that pain, as catalysts for everything I've done since.

I'm not the most talented runner, but I have won against athletes who are better runners than me. Why? Because they got frustrated and gave up. They got tired of losing or of not having a breakthrough, tired of things not lining up, and they stopped trying. They quit.

You know, it only takes a few setbacks to really get someone down and discouraged. When the losses, disappointments, and failures start to pile up, they can cloud everything. Suddenly hindsight simply becomes a list of regrets. And nothing saps your drive and purpose, or undermines success, more than this type of hindsight.

The truth is, we all practice hindsight. And how we do it can either help us or hurt us.

You've probably heard the statement: "What doesn't kill you makes you stronger." That cliché isn't necessarily true, but I have learned that it can be if you have the right perspective, if you practice healthy hindsight.

For me, the right perspective has always been connected to my faith. It's a little like God speaking to my heart on an Olympic track in Beijing, saying, *But you're here.*

If you look back and all you can see is a long list of regrets, it will take you down a road of bitterness and anger. I know this all too well. But if you can look back and find those things you are thankful for, even in the midst of pain and disappointment, your past can become a source of encouragement and empower you to continue running.

I think a healthy hindsight is when you choose to focus on how God loved you, how He was faithful, how He had protected and provided for you.

Yeah, I know, it's easier to look at your past through the lens of disappointment and regret. It actually takes faith to look back through the lens of thankfulness. But I think this is the kind of hindsight that pushes you forward. Another way to write it: you can either let your losses define you, or you can take those losses and use them to motivate you.

While hindsight is twenty-twenty, the truth is, if I actually went back and gave my younger self a cheat sheet, I wouldn't be where I am now.

If I could talk to my younger self today, I wouldn't tell her, "Hey, one day you're going to be a three-time Olympian. You're going to be one of the ten athletes in the history of the United States who competes in the Summer and Winter Games." Instead, I'd tell her, "Don't quit."[4]

Why? Because that young girl had everything she needed to succeed.

My younger self may not know what she would accomplish, but she had a desire and a drive. The fact is, not knowing whether she could become an Olympic athlete was why she did the extra abs workouts and sprints, and why she kept saying no to that beautiful bowl of mint chocolate chip ice cream.

That younger girl doubted whether she was talented enough to even make one team, let alone three, so she couldn't afford to slack off in any area. That girl dreamed of a future, and that dream drove her.

As frustrating as the hurdles of life are, they're important. They help define us. I think it takes a certain amount of losing, a certain number of setbacks, to rev us up, to push us to want it more, to make us more determined. And how we handle those setbacks is everything.

My advice for anyone facing extreme odds, for anyone chasing their dreams? Practice thankfulness, trust God, and don't quit. Just don't quit. Try again, and then try again, and then again.

When you first learn to hurdle, you start off with one. As you get stronger, the coach will add a second, then a third, and so on until you are racing full speed over ten hurdles. One life hurdle gets you stronger for the next challenge and the next.

That's my advice. It's really simple, some might even say cliché, but it's true, and powerfully so. Because we're all gonna lose, we're all gonna fail, and we're all gonna hit a hurdle along the way. Just don't throw in the towel. And when you want to, find something or someone to be thankful for, trust God, and then go pick yourself back up and try again.

How you leave one thing is how you enter the next. How you cross your finish line is how you enter your next race. Because there are no cheat sheets, and you don't get a say in where you are born or those early years of your life or what resources you have access to.

But you're here . . . and there is something to be said for that.

BUT YOU'RE HERE

When I heard God whispering to me, *But you're here*, as I was fighting back tears on the track in front of the millions watching the Olympics around the world, I sensed the miracle of it all.

And in that moment, I was reminded by a good God that I could choose to live a life that would not be determined by my disappointments.

No, by the grace of God, there is no quitting.

The metaphor of hurdling is a truth we can all harness and apply to our lives.

Setting my focus, moving forward, facing life's hurdles, such as a broken family, poverty, racial inequality, dating, waiting and trusting, injuries, rejection, and betrayal—it's all a part of my faith story, my relationship with God and others.

"Over it" is not just about what's in front of you or where you are going. It's also about where you came from. It's about how you leverage your past—regardless of its hardships, disappointments, trials, and abuses—to propel you into your future. It's about how to keep running, keep trusting, keep growing in faith and love.

"Over it" isn't just about how hard you work to achieve your goals; it's about what you do when you fail at reaching your goals. It's about practicing thankfulness. It's about forgiveness. It's about learning how to trust. Yeah, mostly it's about learning how to trust, how to believe, how to have faith, so you can experience a success that is greater than your achievements.

Success has to be greater than an achievement. I say this because, while I have been in three Olympics, I have never medaled. Let me say that again. I'm a three-time Olympian with no Olympic medals. And that really sucks.

But I've learned that success can't be determined by achieving a particular goal, whether it's an Olympic medal, financial freedom, a husband, kids, a house, or a certain career. No. Success is determined by how I live every moment. Success is the state of my heart.

Over It is my life story, my thesis on overcoming and living a successful life.

Poverty? Over it.

Broken family? Over it.

Inequality? Over it.

The 2008 Olympics? Over it.

Overcoming spinal surgery to reach the 2012 Olympics? Over it.

Dating and waiting? So over it!

Rejection from teammates? Over it.

I don't have all the answers. In fact, in this book I'll probably even raise a few questions, because my story is still in progress.

But I do know one thing: I am confident that "he who began a good work in [me] will carry it on to completion until the day of Christ Jesus" (Philippians 1:6).

God is faithful, even when I am not.

Over It. That's the title of this book in which I share about the days I didn't quit and the days I did, and how God has been faithful to complete His good work in me, how He has given me the strength to try again. This is a faith story, and like all faith stories, it's exciting, heartbreaking, hopeful, exhausting, and ultimately about trust. And it's still ongoing.

While I knelt breathless and devastated on an Olympic stage, competing with the world's best, I looked back to four years earlier when I was crying in an apartment while watching others compete in the Olympics. And I realized I was blessed.

But I could have looked even further back, to the girl from Des Moines, Iowa—the quiet, gap-toothed, poor, biracial girl from a fractured family—and realized the odds were never in my favor.

TWO

DAD (MY FIRST COACH) AND FORGIVENESS

My dad taught me how to shoplift because, well, he was a criminal. There's a right way to do it. A practiced, precise way to achieve your goals, to become great. And I was a great shoplifter, for a grade-schooler.

"You're a small fifth grader. Use that to your advantage," Dad said. Dad was my first coach, and that was one of many shoplifting instructions he gave me and my brothers. I love my Dad. He is fun and funny, and it was easy—at least for me, his youngest girl—to listen and earnestly follow his instructions.

Instruction number one: *Use what you've got.*

Most of my shoplifting years were between fourth and sixth grade. I was young, cute, and innocent, and I used those qualities to my advantage. Most people don't suspect you when you're young, cute, and innocent.

Suspicions don't start rising until you're a teenager. My best advice: Don't be a teenager.

Instruction number two: *Wear a coat* (or grow up in Des Moines, Iowa). Yeah, it's easier to shoplift in the brutal cold of a Des Moines winter.

Even a rookie shoplifter can get a couple of candy bars up a bulky coat sleeve. I don't want to come off like I'm bragging, but in my sixth-grade prime, I could steal five candy bars at once. Which leads to . . .

Instruction number three, and this one is important: *Be decisive; no wasted movements.*

You don't *pick up* a candy bar, and you never put it in your pocket. That's amateur hour. Why? Because picking up a candy bar is glaringly obvious; also, and more importantly, it's wasted movement. And putting it in your pocket? That's the first place they look!

No, to steal a candy bar, you simply hover your hand over the Butterfinger and then slide it up your sleeve in one precise, thought-out, hidden movement.

To be a successful shoplifter, you must clearly define your goal and then fearlessly execute it. The more flawless your execution, the greater your success.

After stealing candy bars—and I stole more than a few—I went on to stealing TV dinners. You know you're a pro when you can get five TV dinners inside your coat. You see, while my shoplifting skills were often spent on stealing candy, I also stole food. Hungry-Man steak and potatoes dinners with the little brownie. I was all about that. But I'd also lift mac and cheese or a can of soup, though that was much harder. When I think back, I realize how hungry we all must have been, because, well, what kid steals TV dinners for her family?

A hungry kid.

This leads to another instruction: Do you remember the large bubble mirrors in the ceiling corners of the freezer isle? "Always check those mirrors," Dad said.

One day my dad, my older brothers, Charles and James, my younger brother, Troy, and I were sitting in our car outside a grocery store. (My older sister, Angie, was not with us. She was living with our grandmother at the time.) I was in sixth grade, at the peak of my shoplifting career.

"Listen up," Dad said. "I'm going to get on the pay phone in the store. I'm gonna make a long-distance call to your aunt Chrissy. While I am on the phone, I want you to go into the store, and I want you to steal two or three different things."

So we all went into the store. We spread out while my dad went to the pay phone to make the call.

I was shoplifting, following all the rules: young, cute, and inno-cent; bulky coat; precise, thought-out, hidden movements; checking the mirrors. I stole a comic book, *Wonder Woman*, and a leash for my dad's dog. Dad always had a dog.

So we were all getting it done when Dad gave us the signal and hung up the phone. It was time to go. I walked out of the store, all calm and cute, and joined my dad and two of my brothers at the car. (This was one of the few times we had a car that ran.)

I think it was my youngest brother who walked out of the store last, followed by an irate store manager.

"Sir," the manager yelled to get my dad's attention. "Is this your kid?"

My dad nodded.

"I think he's been stealing," the manager said angrily.

Without missing a beat, my dad turned on my brother and, with a serious dad tone, asked, "Is this true?" followed by "Give back what-ever you took right now!"

As my brother handed over his pilfered candy, Dad turned back to the manager. With a disappointed but serious demeanor, he said, "I am glad you told me. I can't wait till I get him home. He's gonna get the spanking of his life!"

The manager, apparently feeling like justice would be served and that maybe he had played a role in a teachable moment, nodded and let us go. As he returned to the grocery store, the rest of us continued to get in the car with our stolen loot. The manager was hardly out of earshot when my dad looked at my brother who had been caught and said, "Okay, so next time you can't stay in the store so long."

It was a teachable moment for sure, a learning opportunity. And Dad was always good at turning the crazy, and even difficult circumstances, into teachable moments.

HUSTLING

I remember driving home one winter night when the car broke down. Actually, I remember all our cars breaking down, and one time, outside the dentist's office, our car being on fire.

My dad was always finding cheap cars, and they were always breaking down. We could never afford to fix them, so for most of my childhood, we walked or we ran.

It was an icy night in Iowa. It was snowing and there were blizzard warnings. We didn't have any family or friends who could come pick us up, so, you guessed it: teachable moment. We were on foot, and to stay warm, we had to run. I remember Dad telling me how to run correctly so that I could keep my body heat up. I think it was my first running lesson, but it was not my last.

I remember running with my dad from the gas station, the corner store, the grocery store. While we were running, he would coach me on how to control my breathing so I could keep running faster. I loved it—both the quality coaching time with Dad and the running.

When I wasn't running with my dad, I was walking.

But then I was running again.

Elementary school, middle school, and high school, no matter how far the school was, I never got a ride, even when the car was working. It wasn't the typical situation at my house, where Mom and Dad made sure one way or another we were getting to school. Mom and Dad were always working one or two jobs each. So in my house, if we wanted to go to school, rain or shine, snow or ice, wind chills in the minus degrees, we walked to school or we ran.

The closest of the six schools I attended was at least a mile away. Walking took a long time; it was easier and warmer to just run. Plus, if it meant I could sleep in a little longer, well, that was never a bad thing.

I would run one block, and then I'd walk. Then I'd run one block, then walk, which is kinda funny because that's a lot of what my Olympic workouts are today: sprint for twenty seconds, then walk for twenty seconds, and repeat, repeat, repeat until I puke. Apparently I was doing workouts in middle school, minus the puking.

In middle school I also started playing the cello. Hauling that cello to and from school added a whole new element to the workout. I had played the violin before the cello. I should've stuck with the violin, but, hey, I was getting great running and strength training without even knowing it!

"Didn't you have a bike?" you might ask. Stolen.

Don't feel too bad for me, though. My brothers had actually stolen that bike for me. And, of course, we couldn't afford a bike lock.

Walking and running were my primary modes of transportation. So, in an odd way, "Thanks for buying cheap cars, Dad."

When Dad wasn't buying cheap cars, he was hustling. Dad was always hustling to make money; that is, when he wasn't in jail.

Dad was a con man, and I was always intrigued by this. There was one particular hustle, when Dad was on parole, that he involved us in.

Our church, the Salvation Army, gave him a job as a handyman and janitor. I remember they would buy boxes of candy bars that they would let the kids sell to raise money so they could go to summer Bible school camps. These programs were for kids like us who otherwise couldn't afford summer camps.

I don't know how Dad was able to get his hands on those boxes of candy bars from the Salvation Army church without them noticing, but he was a criminal and, most of the time, a pretty good one.

Dad decided to employ the same business strategy for selling the candy bars, because if it ain't broke, don't fix it, right?

And it worked. Not wanting to sell them too close to home, Dad would drive my brothers and me to Iowa State University, about thirty minutes from Des Moines. We would knock on every fraternity, sorority, and surrounding neighborhood door.

Door to door, for hours, we sold overpriced candy bars to rich kids and older white people. We told them we were selling candy bars to raise money for a school trip or a basketball team, which wasn't actually a lie, at least not completely. We were trying to raise money, and the cause of helping my family survive was a good one.

The story would change because we were kids and we'd get mixed up, but one thing Dad never let us do was incorporate the church into our story. Dad was never a religious man, but he was a God-fearing man. So, while selling stolen candy bars from the church to raise money for some fake charity was okay, it was crossing a line if we mentioned the church in our pitch. I know it doesn't make sense, but if you think about it, most religious rules don't make sense.

Anyway, it was an easy sale. The people seemed eager to buy the candy bars. I think they felt bad for us because, first, it was cold and, second, we were cute.

We worked hard! And it was worth it just to be in on one of Dad's schemes. Plus, on the way home he would treat us to a Kentucky Fried Chicken dinner. We never got to go out to eat, so going to KFC was like winning the lottery.

Dad mostly used the money to pay our mortgage, our heat bill, and our water bill, or to buy food. Mostly.

Sometimes I think he used it for drinks.

You see, my dad is a good man who raised us to be street-smart. He did his best. It was what he knew and therefore what he could teach us. He can be encouraging, generous, and fun. He is also hilarious, probably one of the funniest people I know. And he has always been one of my biggest inspirations.

But most of the memories that support these sentiments, and all the stories you just read, are from the part of my childhood that came after my dad served seven years of a nine-year prison sentence for nearly beating Mom to death.

A RELATIONSHIP WITH MY DAD

Dad drank, and when he did, all hell could break lose. There was violence. Never with us kids, but between my mom and dad.

I was six, so the memory of the day my dad nearly killed my mom is vague, but the emotions are not. It was a day of chaos, fear, and sadness.

We couldn't afford a phone in the house, but we lived next to a park with a pay phone. The image of my sister running across a field is imprinted on my mind; she was running to the phone to call 911. Running to save Mom.

Then there were a lot of policemen and paramedics and more chaos and fear.

To this day I know only a few details. My family doesn't talk about it. When I last asked my mom about it, she simply said, "It was a fight. I ended up going to the hospital."

That's the day Mom, battered and broken, was fighting for her life, and soon after, Dad went to prison. I don't know what the official charges were, but I know she was in the hospital for weeks. I know he nearly killed her. And I know our lives got even harder after that.

I have been asked if I've forgiven my dad. It's a fair question. I guess I have, but I was young and mostly sheltered from the bad things he did. Dad could be violent with my brothers. He spanked them much harder than he should have, but he was never violent with me, maybe because I am a girl. In many ways, even though his actions clearly affected my life, I've never known him as a bad man. A flawed man, yes; absent, yes; but not evil.

So, if forgiving Dad means I recognize that I grew up in the dysfunctional reality of my parents' broken lives, if it means I acknowledge how he failed my mom and us in many ways, then yes, I have forgiven him. But because I have never wrestled with unforgiveness, anger, or bitterness toward him, I have no need to forgive him for those things. I am not saying I've never wrestled with unforgiveness, anger, or bitterness, because I have. Just not with my dad.

It surprises some people to hear that I never had a moment where I had to make a conscious decision to forgive my dad. I think it's because I grew up forgiving him. He is my dad, and I love him.

My love for both my parents is very deep, and I think it's a very godlike love. But so many people don't seem to get it.

Years ago, a *TMZ* reporter met me at an airport and asked what I thought about justice, forgiveness, law and order, and the nature of punishment in our world today. I know, heady stuff for *TMZ*.

> **Reporter:** I just wanted to ask you one question if you don't mind.

I was walking toward the exit and thought, a little sarcastically, *Oh, good*, TMZ.

> **Reporter:** Well, first of all, I just want to say sorry about what happened with *Dancing with the Stars*. How are you doing? . . . Are you . . .

He paused, and I laughed.

> **Me:** Have I emotionally recovered from *Dancing with the Stars*? Pretty sure I have.

It was true, by the way. I had. I mean, I did spend my entire life training for *Dancing with the Stars*, so the loss was devastating but . . . wait, never mind. I was thinking about something else I had spent my entire life training for.

Then the reporter's next question surprised me.

Reporter: Obviously, you're an Olympian. Your fellow Olympian Oscar Pistorius just got [sentenced] to five years. I was just wondering how you felt about that. . . .

Me: I didn't really stay [up-to-date] with much of the trial. . . .

I hadn't. But I did know that Oscar Pistorius, a former South African Olympian, had been on trial for the murder of his girlfriend, Reeva Steenkamp.

Me: It's hard for me because I actually have a dad who was in prison for murder. . . . [I left out the part that it was for nearly killing my mom.] So I am one of the most nonjudgmental people on people . . . who are struggling.

I am not a judge, I wasn't on the jury, and I had absolutely nothing to do with the case. So in one sense it was really strange to be asked what I thought about the sentencing of Oscar Pistorius. However, we live in a day when people are fascinated with crime and absolutely obsessed with the punishment. We love to talk about it, to give our two cents' worth. And since I am an Olympian, I guess it made perfect sense to a *TMZ* reporter to stop me for a sound bite.

Me: There's two sides to the story. . . . I know on one end there's the [Steenkamp] family who's suffering, and then you have Oscar as well. . . . It's in God's hands. . . . For me, as a Christian, God is my ultimate judge. . . . All I can just say is . . . you just have to keep the family in your prayers, for sure, because they lost their daughter. And you have to keep Oscar in your prayers . . . [so] that in prison he rehabs and has great counseling.[1]

I was nearly crucified on social media for that last statement. People couldn't understand how I could pray for Oscar. I get it. Oscar was found guilty of murder. He is the cause of great pain and suffering. He is paying a price for it, and rightly so.

But I also know from experience that while he needs to face the consequences of his crime, while there is nothing he can do to change his past or ease the suffering he's caused, if he repents, he can know God's love and forgiveness and salvation.

I believe God forgives and saves.

This is not a theory or a hope. I know this to be true in light of my childhood and my relationship with my dad.

A couple of years after the TMZ backlash, I was similarly criticized for posting an image on Instagram of me and Floyd Mayweather, who three years earlier had served three months for domestic violence.[2]

This time I responded to the social media backlash by telling my story about the power of forgiveness and salvation. I posted, "My dad domestically abused my mother. He almost killed her. She was in the hospital for months. He served many years in jail."

I wanted to be clear that Jesus forgives, and we can know this forgiveness if we repent.

I had seen and experienced this in my life and also with my dad, so I continued, "Jesus saved him. He never laid hands on her again." And finally, "God calls us to forgive. We all fall short. We all sin."[3]

This is the foundation of my faith. Jesus died on a cross so I could be set free from the shame and condemnation of my sin.

He died for *every* person's sin, so every person might know forgiveness and salvation.

He hung on that cross for the whole world because He loves us. And when He cried out on the cross, "Father, forgive them, for they do not know what they are doing" (Luke 23:34), He extended His forgiveness to everyone.

That may not seem fair, but if you're the sinner, it's the difference between life and death.

There isn't a sin God doesn't forgive. And when we repent, when we ask God to forgive and save and change us, we can know this forgiveness, we can be saved, and we can be changed.

I am not suggesting there aren't consequences to sin. Romans 6:23 states: "The wages of sin is death." But that's only the first half of the verse. The rest of that verse is: "But the gift of God is eternal life in Christ Jesus our Lord." Wouldn't it be amazing if we were just as familiar with the second half of the verse?

God's forgiveness provides a road back to life.

I once heard a preacher say, "You can't give away what you don't have."

I have been forgiven. I am learning how to give it away. Unforgiveness is one of the most important hurdles I have had to overcome. To this day, there are so many reasons why I am working on this. But I am convinced there is no going forward if I can't forgive those who have hurt me in the past.

When people criticized me, asking how I could post a picture with Mayweather, I responded, "If I can't take a picture with him, I guess I should remove the pictures of my dad in my home as well."[4]

You know, if I wasn't willing to forgive someone who has done terrible things, then I wouldn't have a relationship with my dad.

FORGIVE

I started this chapter by telling some of my favorite dad stories. Some of them involved activities that weren't even legal. I have learned how to look back on my dad and our relationship when I was growing up and find the things that were good. I chose to start with those stories so you'd understand why I feel about him the way I do now.

I wanted you to see a man who, even though he was deeply flawed, was also sincere and generous, and someone I deeply loved as a child. And still do. I wanted you to see him the way I see him, as a good man who has struggled with his demons, a man God has forgiven, a man God loves, a man who has changed.

I knew if I started with the story of Dad beating Mom, you might not have been able to see past his abuse, past the brokenness and trauma of what he did. Then you might not have been able to enjoy his humor, his encouragement, his positive approach to frustrating or hard circumstances. And you would have missed his brilliant problem-solving mind and his creative, albeit illegal, methods for providing for his family's needs, which are all things that formed me.

As I said, my dad was my first coach.

Without my dad I would not be the person I am today. I am thankful for the good things.

Don't misunderstand. Our lives were hard after Dad went to prison. And it marked my life and the lives of my mom and siblings in many ways.

Dad wasn't there for me very often, and yes, that's sometimes still hard to deal with. But I am learning how to forgive. Does it mean forget? Of course not. Does it mean trust? Not necessarily. That's ultimately his responsibility. But it does open my heart to the possibility.

Mostly—and this is what I am all about—it frees me to run, to pursue my goals without the baggage of unforgiveness. It's hard enough to hurdle life's obstacles without having to drag my fatherless years with me everywhere I go.

To anyone reading this who also has a traumatic past, I want to say, "That sucks and I'm sorry you had to go through that. But here's what I have learned: there's a way to heal, to move forward, and it's through forgiveness."

I have felt God's challenge to forgive in so many areas of my life. I'm not perfect at it; when someone hurts me, I don't want to forgive. But I know what it is like to be forgiven by God. And His kindness and love are what ultimately inspire me to forgive.

I have learned that in order to hurdle that broken place where I have been wronged, I have to choose to forgive. I am not saying forget. I am not saying trust. I am saying forgive. I've learned that there is great freedom on the other side of forgiveness.

Choosing to forgive is not always easy. I know this all too well, especially in other areas of my life, which we'll get to. But I know this too: the need to judge and punish someone is its own prison. Unforgiveness will keep you from achieving your goals. So even if you don't feel it, if you want to experience any type of future that isn't being haunted by a broken past, forgive. Every day, choose to forgive.

THE END OF MY SHOPLIFTING CAREER

There were days when shoplifting determined what was for dinner. At the time, for me, it wasn't a matter of right and wrong; it was a matter of needs being met.

I learned from my dad that sometimes you do what you must to provide for your family. He taught me how to be street-smart and tough. He also taught me what was right and wrong. Maybe most of that was from Mom, but Dad had a sense of street justice that served me well. Ultimately it led me to retire from my shoplifting career.

In high school, I'd sometimes go to the mall to hang out with a girl from my school. She started shoplifting clothes, and I was disgusted by it for two reasons. First, she didn't need clothes. Second, she was really bad at shoplifting.

Seeing her do it made me realize how stupid it was. I never shoplifted again after that, not even for food, although our family was still pretty poor. By then, I was old enough to get a job, so I did.

So, yeah, I retired from shoplifting.

THREE

MOM, POVERTY, AND LEARNING TO WORK

In elementary school we had what the teachers called a "fun run." *Fun* and *run* in the same sentence? Clearly my teachers had a grasp of the obvious; at least, obvious to me. I think it was third grade when everyone had to run at least one lap around the playground at recess. You know, to "get some exercise." After the lap we were free to play, or—and this may be the best use of the word *or*—we could keep running laps.

Yeah, how cool was that?

But it gets even better!

With each lap we would be given a ticket. So we could essentially spend our entire recess working to win tickets. Amazing, right?

But it gets even better than that. There was a prize!

Actually, there were prizes, plural. The more tickets we earned, the more options we had when it came to picking the prizes.

As you can imagine, we all gladly traded our playing time during recess so we could run laps.

Okay, maybe I was the only kid who ran the entire recess. For me it was about the prizes. I loved to win prizes. Even now, give me a shot at a prize, an award, and I will compete.

There is something beautifully simple about competing—against myself or another person—for the fastest time or the latest record. Also, there is a sense of stability in running. You can control your pace; you can push or back off.

The world makes the most sense to me when there is a clear objective and a goal to achieve. The world of pushing myself is a world I thrive in.

But not everything in this world is so straightforward . . .

HOW LORI MET JAMES

If you catch Mom on the right day, she will tell you how she met Dad.

"He had green eyes," she says. "And a nice build," she adds without prompting.

"Whoa, Mom. Maybe more on how you met and less on how attractive he was," I say, even though I enjoy it.

"Oh, I was downtown one day waiting for the bus. And he invited me over to his apartment for a chicken dinner. He said, 'I'm gonna cook some chicken. Would you like to come over and eat with me?' And I said, 'Oh, well, I guess.' And that's how it all started. With a chicken dinner."

I nod. I've had Dad's chicken dinner.

As if Mom reads my thoughts, she continues, "He was an excellent cook and baker!"

"Yes, he was, and he could make something out of nothing. Two-day-old leftovers were an exciting meal when he was done cooking. Even beans tasted good when he made them," I say in agreement.

Mom nods. "That was one of his good qualities." She pauses reflectively, and I know there's a world of pain in what she doesn't say.

This is harder for me than I thought it would be, but I keep us moving forward with a question I know the answer to: "What was the age difference between you both?"

"He was in the Korean War when I was a baby," Mom says. "He was about twenty years older than me. But he was one of those good-looking men who age well. He was like Richard Gere. Got better with age."

I shake my head; there she goes again.

As volatile as their relationship was, Mom can still talk about Dad and smile. And as complicated as my relationship with her has been at times, I appreciate that about her.

Dad moved in with Mom and her two other children shortly after that chicken dinner, but they never got married. Whenever I've asked Mom about it, she simply says, "He didn't want to."

What I *can* tell you is that the instability of their relationship and the negative impact it had on our family played a role in my decision to remain a virgin until I got married.

After they moved in together, Dad became more than just a stepfather to my oldest siblings, Angie and Charles. He became Dad. He always treated them like his own, and while each of us has had our own unique relational complications with him, all five of us kids have a relationship with Dad.

Mom and Dad had three more kids: James, Lori (that's me), and Troy.

Over the first five years of my life, before he went to prison, Dad was in and out of jail. I don't know exactly what for. I think petty crime mostly, though I know he robbed a bank before he met Mom.

I know this because it was my favorite bedtime story. It was a funny one for a couple of reasons. First, he got caught because he wore high-ankle pants, which was the style at the time. The lady he blindfolded could see his ankles, and my dad was the only black guy in the town. Second, while my dad could explain in detail the bank robbery, he couldn't tell us where the money went. That's because he forgot where he buried it. How is that possible? Every country road and farm look the same in Missouri.

Moral of the story: criminals have the best bedtime stories.

THE PIZZA PRIZE

In 1989, when I was in second grade, Pizza Hut had this great initiative they started with school systems nationwide called BOOK IT! Its goal was to urge kids to read, and the prize was pizza.

When I looked this up, I couldn't believe it's still a thing. I literally pulled these rules from their website: "Set a reading goal for each child in your class. When they meet their monthly goal, you get to recognize them with a Reading Award Certificate, good for a free one-topping Personal Pan Pizza."[1]

It was one of my favorite things as a child because I loved to read. Most of my childhood we didn't have TV, and the times we did, there was nothing good to watch on it. So reading became my obsession. I could disappear into a story for hours at a time.

"You always kept to yourself," Mom said. "I always knew when your brothers were in the house. They made a lot of noise, but you were always quiet. If there was too much noise, and there was always too much noise, you would find an empty room with your cat, Whiskers, and read a book. You were an easy child."

It'd been a long time since I'd thought about our long-whiskered cat.

I was an advanced reader because, well, you know the saying, "Anything worth doing, do it until you're the best at it," or something like that.

So I was reading one-thousand-page Stephen King books by fifth grade. *Needful Things* was a pretty intense read. It's about jealousy over other people's possessions and how that can make you go crazy. That book was good and scary and horrible. And looking back, had my mom not been working so much, she probably would not have let her fifth grader read Stephen King novels.

Note to my future mom self: no Stephen King.

But this story is less about Stephen King and more about pizza.

When I learned I could win at reading, and that the prize was pizza, well, is there anything better?

Actually, yes, there is something better: a bigger pizza.

When Pizza Hut started making their "personal" pizza, they did a disservice to the word *personal*. Winning the Personal Pan Pizza from Pizza Hut was probably the first time I was let down as far as awards go. Even a middle schooler can eat it in a few bites.

And I had three brothers.

I remember being so excited and proud to claim and share my hard-earned prize with my family. And when it arrived, I gobbled it down with a smile.

But I have to say, samples at Costco are bigger.

So prizes can let you down. And there's a lesson in that: life isn't always about achieving. But the fact is, while this life is not all about the end prize, there's something powerfully satisfying and empowering and life-giving in the pursuit of a prize.

There is also something assuring and settling in the pursuit, because it's something within my control.

And I think, especially when I was young, I needed something within my control. Because it sucks to be a passenger in an out-of-control car, which, at times, was a good way to describe my childhood. I was looking for a sense of control and security, and in many ways, competition was my way of getting behind the wheel, of driving the car. You see, after Dad nearly killed Mom and went to prison, many of my securities were stripped away, and that's when life got really hard.

Especially for Mom.

JOBLESS AND HOMELESS

When Mom was released from the hospital, she was already behind on the mortgage. Suddenly she was alone; a battered, abandoned, single mom of five who could hardly keep the heat on in the house, let alone pay the mortgage.

"Over that year the bills started piling up—the heat bill, the electric bill. We often didn't have enough money even for food or gas for the car, and then there were the social workers," Mom told me.

From a very young age I remember the social workers at our house. When I asked Mom about it, she said, "It was really scary. I knew they had the power to break up the family. They were constantly dropping in and checking up on me. I did everything I could to keep us all together. But I really needed to work."

I remember this.

Mom was always working or looking for work. Often, we would be left alone at home or in the car. One time, when Mom was looking for work, because of the threat of social workers dropping in, she took us with her. I vaguely remember going downtown to a big, fancy hotel. She sat us down in the lobby and said, "I want you all to sit here and wait till I come back. Don't move. I'll come back."

"Do you remember that, Mom?" I asked.

She barked a laugh. "Yeah, I went down to the basement and talked to a manager about a housekeeping job. The five of you were between the ages of six months and ten years; you were six. I didn't tell the manager I had five kids waiting for me upstairs. I didn't tell her I had no one I could leave you with and nowhere to go."

"Did you get the job?"

Mom laughed again. "Yeah, I got the job!"

I'll come back. That's a good way to describe Mom. She always came back.

Mom had her own struggles, but she worked herself to the bone. She did her best, she tried to protect us from our desperate circumstances, and she always came back.

But she couldn't protect us from everything. She couldn't protect us from poverty.

On the day we lost the house, Mom gave each of us a blanket and put us in the car and just started driving. She drove around with no destination in mind. Over the next few days, we stayed on the floors of friends' apartments until we ended up at the Salvation Army.

The Salvation Army was our home church. I practically grew up there. It was one of the very few things that was consistent in my childhood. Our church community often provided help to my family, but no more so than when they became a home for a homeless family.

They gave Mom the keys to the church building until we found something permanent, and for several weeks we lived in the basement of the Salvation Army, or what my brothers and I called the dungeon. It wasn't a home; it was old tile bathrooms and rubber mats and storage rooms filled with athletic equipment, tables, and chairs. There were temporary army cots and a shower, and we could use the kitchen if we wanted to. It wasn't a home, but it was a lifeline to a homeless mom with kids and nowhere to go.

I remember it well because it was during that part of the summer when the church offered day camps. I loved those camps—day camps, weekend camps, and, my favorite, the weeklong summer camps away from home. I think those were Mom's favorite camps as well.

Camps were fun. There were lots of games, and I got to just play.

My brothers and I would wake up early. It was important to be upstairs in the gym before the other kids got there. First, there was basketball and dodgeball and lots of other fun things to do in the gym. But mostly we didn't want anyone to know our dad was in jail and we were poor and homeless and living downstairs.

When we got there early, it looked like our parents were the first to drop us off at the camp. Which was funny because it was probably the only time I was consistently early to anything.

Much of my childhood was spent trying to hide how poor we were and the sense of shame that came with it. Even though I was six and naive to much of the nuance of our hardship, even though Dad's absence and our homeless circumstances weren't my fault, even though my mom was doing her very best, poverty had a way of making me feel ashamed.

TRACK AND FIELD AND FACING FEAR

I liked sports. All of them. Any extracurricular sports activity, any after-school program, I was there. I played basketball and ran track.

I did every event: the long jump, the mile, the high jump, the 4x400m relay.

And then there was hurdles.

One day my middle school coach approached me and said, "We need a hurdler."

I knew from the girls who had quit the hurdles that they were hard and even dangerous. I knew you could fall and hurt yourself and possibly even scar your legs. But I wasn't afraid.

"I'll do it," I said.

That's the story. There was no epic music, no whispered words from heaven, no sense of destiny, no coach recognizing potential greatness—just a girl who wasn't afraid and needed an opportunity to prove it.

I wasn't afraid; at least, not of falling. I never have been. As it turns out, that is an important temperament for being a good hurdler. It also turns out, I was really good at hurdles. I didn't lose a race that whole season, my first season.

When you find something you are good at, something that makes you come alive, you are truly blessed, and you should do that thing. But track and field was more than just something I was good at; it provided stability, focus, and a sense of security in a world that was unstable, unclear, and often insecure. Track and field offered something I wasn't getting anywhere else: a sense of self-control.

Fearless self-control, the willingness to give everything toward reaching one goal—this has marked my life. This mentality is what set me apart from the other girls on my middle school team.

Maybe the other girls didn't need track and field like I did, or maybe they just didn't want what it offered like I did. Probably a little of both. But my life and personality set me up for the opportunity, and I took it by the horns.

Maybe, because of my early life, I couldn't afford to be afraid of getting hurt. I don't know. The one thing I do know is that sometimes people impede their own success because they are afraid they'll fail or get hurt. Fear is something that has to be faced.

And I faced fear full-on that first season.

The 300-meter hurdles is a painful event to run. You are going to feel lactic acid; you are going to run out of breath and be exhausted; you are going to want to quit. And just thinking of that before the race made me so nervous I would throw up. Every time.

But I faced my fear. Every time.

I learned in those early days that when you hurdle, if you are fearful and back off, it actually affects your momentum and can cause you to hit the hurdle and hurt yourself. The best way to hurdle is to run straight at it. Being timid will tighten your steps and you will not cover as much ground, which will put you in a position to not clear or jump over the hurdle.

No fear is the key to good hurdling. It is the key to getting over the hurdle. It is the key to getting over something blocking your path.

So when the doubt creeps into your mind that the hurdle is too big or you won't make it, do not listen and press on.

While I have never been afraid of falling, I've known fear. It was the fear of failing, of living a life of poverty and shame. I was too young to put words to my fear, but I wasn't too young to face it. Fear was something I harnessed, something I used to motivate myself and push myself forward.

When you hurdle, you have to focus on one hurdle at a time. If you are at the start line and look at all ten hurdles, it can become daunting. It can look like a wave of obstacles that will be too hard to overcome.

I learned that when I focus on only the first hurdle, on getting over that one, the next hurdle becomes less daunting. Hurdle by hurdle is how I keep my momentum. As with hurdling, setting and achieving one goal at a time help me not to become overwhelmed by the circumstances of life.

My childhood was often scary and out of control, but hurdles put the steering wheel in my hands. Running was something within my control.

If I ran the laps or read the books, I was rewarded with a prize. If I sowed, I reaped. If I set a goal and worked hard, I could achieve it. There is something beautiful and true and freeing in sowing into something and then reaping the rewards of your hard work.

FOOD STAMPS AND POVERTY

I can describe the food stamps from my childhood vividly.

They looked a little like money, with the faces of old white men printed on them. But they were colorful and slightly larger than actual bills. Like money, they came in denominations of ones, fives, and tens. But unlike money, the words *Food Coupon* were written boldly on them so no one would accidently feel as though they had earned them.

So, yeah, they looked a little like real money, but they felt like shame. Using them was basically announcing to the whole world, or at least the whole grocery store, which felt like the whole world: "We are really poor and therefore not as respectable as the rest of you."

I remember Mom occasionally sending my brothers and me into the grocery store, each with a dollar food stamp, and giving us instructions to buy a five-cents piece of bubble gum so the cashier had to give us each ninety-five cents in change.

Because that week we were so poor that we needed to work the system to pay for something other than our food.

That week we couldn't afford to pay the rent . . . again.

That week Mom's temp job ended . . . again.

That week we needed gas money for the car . . . again.

That week the heat was turned off, the electricity, the water . . . again.

One time I remember my science teacher came over to our apartment to illegally turn our water back on. The sense of helplessness and shame you feel when your teacher learns how poor you are . . . it marks you, even when you aren't fully aware of it at the time.

The humiliation of how poor we were touched every part of my life, even the parts I was unconscious of until I looked back.

For example, I didn't have a childhood best friend. It's hard to have a best friend when you move from apartment to apartment, from one school district to the next, when you go to six schools in eight years.

I didn't really have any deep friendships. It's hard to make friends when you don't want to invite anyone over to your apartment for a sleepover or playdate because you're afraid they will see how poor you really are. You're afraid they might see roaches or that you have no food or snacks to eat. Because then, you would be really embarrassed and ashamed.

There were so many things my family couldn't afford. I remember a school dance, and my mom couldn't afford to buy me a dress. My first running shoes were a used pair of basketball high-tops that a girl at my school loaned to me. It's really hard to run track in high-tops. My first pair of track spikes were given to me out of the trunk of a car by a parent of another athlete. I was so thankful, but at the same time, angry that we couldn't afford them.

I used them for the whole track season.

GOD IS FAITHFUL; I CAN PROVE IT

Growing up poor is hard. It touches every aspect of life: social, relational, and physical. I know the hardship, pain, embarrassment, and shame that often come with poverty.

But why does poverty feel so shameful? I think it's because poverty is a form of injustice.

Several years ago I created the Lolo Jones Foundation, a nonprofit dedicated to helping single mothers, families with incarcerated loved ones, and poverty-stricken communities. I feel passionately about the injustice of poverty.

Once I started doing two sports, track and bobsled, it became really hard to host functions for my foundation. But the last event we did, we gave kids a shopping spree at Academy Sports. No donated used shoes out of trunks for these kids. They got to go around the store and pick out athletic shoes and gear. And all the kids were from families where a parent was incarcerated.

I believe God hates poverty. Poverty tries to steal dignity and self-respect from a person and, with them, their future. But Jesus taught that every person is valuable and worthy. He treated the poor with love, dignity, and respect. He ministered to the most oppressed. And He taught us to do the same. Jesus said, "Whatever you [do] for one of the least of these brothers and sisters of mine, you [do] for me" (Matthew 25:40). He was talking about the poor, the hungry, and the thirsty. My family experienced this kind of ministry from our church and so many generous people along the way.

The fact is, I grew up poor, and I couldn't do anything about that. The other fact is, people helped us, and I could do something about that.

I would have much rather that we had the money to buy shoes, but we didn't. So when those shoes were given to me, I had a choice to make: see them as a handout that highlighted and cemented my socioeconomic status and embrace the shame so often associated with poverty, or see them as an opportunity to put away the shame and earn them by running my hardest every day.

Yes, poverty is an injustice. But one of the ways I have discovered freedom from this injustice is to take hold of what I have been given and work harder than the person next to me.

If I could have earned enough to buy those shoes myself, I would have; instead, they were given to me. So, with gratitude, I took them and used them to earn the next pair. It's back to sowing and reaping, to hard work. As much as I believe those who have should seek to bless those who have not, you don't get out of poverty through gifts alone. Breaking out of poverty is nearly impossible without community, but it's absolutely impossible without hard work.

I might not have been an Olympian today if someone hadn't given me those shoes when we couldn't afford to buy a pair. But I most certainly would not be an Olympian today if I hadn't taken those shoes and then run hard every day since.

My point is that God, through people, has been faithful to me, and I have worked hard to partner my hard work with their generosity. I agree with James who said, "Every good and perfect gift is from above, coming down from the Father of the heavenly lights, who does not change like shifting shadows" (James 1:17).

Here's my encouragement: sometimes if you want to hurdle your unjust circumstances, hardships, and unfair experiences, it's as simple as recognizing where God has been faithful, and then working hard to prove His faithfulness.

Okay, maybe it's not simple. But I do believe anyone can work hard. It doesn't guarantee that you will reach your goal; it's more about what it forms in you, who you can become along the way.

And here is another encouragement: if you have an extra pair of shoes in your trunk, give them to that kid who needs them.

You never know, maybe that kid will become the next Olympic hurdler.

A COACH AND A WORK ETHIC

When people ask me, "Where do you get the strength to fight again? Where do you get your motivation?" I tell them, "The Salvation Army church played no small part in instilling core values in me as a child. Not only did they help us by giving us shelter and food, but they helped on the spiritual side as well."

That's true. But when it comes to track and field, it wasn't just church that helped. There were a handful of people along the way, parents and girls who loaned me high-tops or spikes and the coaches who believed in me.

Many articles and documentaries have been published on my

formative track and field days, but none of them highlights the person who had the greatest impact on me. It's time for me to set things straight, because too often the person who most influenced an athlete isn't recognized. It happens more than you might think. The names credited for an athlete's success are often inflated, then narratives are written, and they become well-worn paths until the true story about the humble, quietly hardworking, self-sacrificing coaches are forgotten.

So let me give some credit where credit is due . . .

My high school coach was great, but he didn't know about hurdles. So he turned me over to the men's hurdle coach. But that coach didn't have time for me; his son was projected to get a scholarship in hurdles, so he was solely focused on the boys. I was left to figure things out by myself.

But in the summer between my freshman and sophomore years, I met Coach Phil Ferguson.

Ferguson was a summer track coach, and his workouts made athletes quit summer track. He wasn't a hurdles coach either—I actually never had a hurdles coach until college—but he taught me the fundamentals.

Most of the work in track and field, especially at the beginning of a season, isn't hurdling. At first, it's all about getting a base of running. So I would run sprint workouts, I would get my strength up, and I would do drills. His workouts were really tough, especially for high school. I mean, my first workouts where I threw up were with him. He definitely pushed his athletes. For a high school coach, he was one of the best I ever had.

He was also one of those coaches who wasn't in it purely for the sport; he had a desire to help kids stay on the straight and narrow. He tried to help kids stay focused and out of trouble during the summer months. He was a good man, a solid Christian, a man of God. He wove his faith into the foundation of sports. We would pray on the bus, and we all knew we could trust him.

And he was balanced. We had hard days, but there were also days that made us appreciate the sport.

Then there was the opportunity to travel.

I loved to travel; I still do. A chance to be anywhere that wasn't Iowa was very exciting.

Coach Ferguson knew how appetizing the opportunity to travel was to his athletes, so he made us work for it. Only the best traveled, which deepened my desire to make the travel team. And I did.

The Des Moines Area Youth Track Club was our name. We all hated it. It was too long and barely fit on our track uniforms. Plus, it was hard to recite after a race. When we were tired and winded, someone would always ask what team we ran for. Yeah, we all hated the name. But we all loved to be on the team.

We traveled and competed all around the United States. We went to Texas, Washington, and New York.

Looking back, I realize that the lessons I've learned from track over the last twenty years began in earnest in those early days with Coach Ferguson and the Des Moines Area Youth Track Club:

1. Work for it.
2. Fight through pain or discomfort.
3. Losing can be winning.
4. Don't quit. (I won because others quit.)
5. Don't listen to doubts or fears.
6. Shortcuts lead to poverty. (Proverbs 21:5 says, "The plans of the diligent lead to profit as surely as haste leads to poverty.")

I learned that if you outwork the athlete next to you, you can earn new and exciting experiences. I learned how to set goals, how to work hard and reap the rewards. I learned that you can have a chance to reap only if you sow. You may not always win, at least not the way you want, but without sowing, without putting in the work, nothing changes.

This is one of the most important lessons I needed to learn as a track athlete, because winning is never going to come easy. You have to be willing to work for it. And not just on the track but off it as well. Because for a track and field athlete, you have to earn your spot physically and also earn your way financially.

Those travel meets? They cost money, and I didn't have any. But Coach Ferguson would let us know how much we would need and then organize fundraising opportunities. On occasion he found donors, but in the end, each of us had to raise most of the money. We all had to put in the work.

I spent hours outside grocery stores by myself selling raffle tickets for a free grocery shopping trip. Coach would help set up the table and the signs, but selling the tickets was on me. I would sit outside the store entrance and refine my sales pitch until I had perfected it. I would get about twenty noes for every yes, and then someone would throw me a dollar bill.

I knew I was raising money so I could participate in a future travel meet. But what I didn't know was how much training I was getting for a future as a professional track and field athlete. While I only needed to raise $500 for my high school meets, it costs a whole lot more to become a professional athlete.

Whether you're in high school or an adult, money doesn't come out of thin air.

So essentially, those summers when I was raffling off tickets and getting twenty noes for every yes, I was learning a valuable skill for my future.

MOM AND A FUTURE

When I look at my parents, I see complicated layers of sincere love and codependency.

My mom loved my dad and vice versa. It was a love that, at times, was built on a meeting of mutual needs, but it was still love.

When Dad got out of prison, Mom wanted to reunite the family and be with him. So he came home. By then I was in high school and well on my way toward earning a college scholarship.

Dad did his best to take up the reins of providing for the family. But with a criminal record, it was hard for him to find or keep a job. Eventually he found a job in a smaller town in Iowa, which meant my family had to move. But moving would have required me to give up my track and field participation, because the school in the new town didn't have a track team. This meant I would be off the radar for colleges. And that wasn't an option for me.

I had set a goal and worked hard, and a scholarship was the prize.

"I knew you were good," Mom told me. "I remember you running at Drake University in Des Moines, and the college coaches there showed a lot of interest in you. It was the first time I thought you must be really good. I was having a lot of money problems and a lot of problems with your dad. I was beside myself. But I knew you went to a good high school, and I hoped you could get a scholarship."

It was good to hear Mom share this with me. That last year of high school was hard because my entire family moved to another town, and I stayed in Des Moines.

"It was really hard to leave you," Mom said. "But I knew we didn't have anything to offer you." Hearing her say those words brought up painful memories. Dad had wanted me to move with the family, but I disagreed and told Mom, "I can't go to a city that doesn't have track."

Mom agreed. She went to Coach Ferguson and asked if there was a family I could stay with for my last year of high school. I ended up staying with the Essex family. Their younger son ran distance on the Des Moines Area Youth Track Club with me in the summer.

"I know that last year was hard, but when we left Des Moines, we ended up bouncing from motel to motel before finding an apartment. If you had come with us, you wouldn't have had a track team, and if we'd found a school with one, you would have had to start all over with track and coaches. It would have been difficult," Mom said.

And she was right. I wouldn't be where I am today if I hadn't stayed and finished out at my high school. Track and field was my way out of poverty. I knew it, and Mom did as well. And she did what she could, as she always has, to help me achieve my goals.

I started getting recruitment letters from all over the country: Harvard, University of Texas, Columbia. Schools that had seen my track results were offering scholarships.

I could go anywhere. I was the first in my family to go to college and graduate. It was a huge step toward breaking the cycle of poverty.

You know, you don't choose your family. You don't choose your financial status. You don't get a say in where you're born or what parents you're born to or siblings you'll spend the most formative part of your life with. You don't get a say in whether you're white or black or what natural gifts you're given. You also don't get a say in whether you will be a recipient of someone else's generosity. But you can choose how hard you will work with what you have been given.

Poverty was an obstacle I had to hurdle on my way to becoming a professional athlete and an Olympian. And poverty is a cruel thief. It will try to steal your value and your future. It will leave you feeling helpless and embarrassed and fearful. But I have learned that you can reject the injustice of poverty through community, thankfulness, and hard work.

I am a statistical anomaly. I beat the odds. I didn't do it alone, but I also didn't do it sitting down. Your circumstances can either define your limitations or prepare you to overcome them. It all depends on how much work you're willing to put in.

So fight the injustices of your past, scorn the shame, take what you've been given, put in the work, and get over it.

CHALLENGE ACCEPTED

It was a cloudy day, but otherwise beautiful. I stood on the edge of the track breathless and scared about my future. It was 2004, and I was a college senior at my first Olympic trials. At that moment, it felt as if it was my last as well.

In the qualifying round I placed ninth with a time of 12.93. I lost by one-hundredth of a second to Danielle Carruthers, who clocked in at 12.92. It was the closest finish in the semifinals that year. One-hundredth of a second—you can't even snap your fingers in that time frame.

Danielle ended up missing out on the Olympic team by the same margin in the finals, finishing fourth by a margin of one-hundredth of a second.

But for Danielle, who had already signed a Nike sponsorship, her performance set her up to be able to compete in Europe that year while I stayed home.

I was out.

Crying on the grass field next to the warm-up track, I thought my career was over before it even had a chance to start. I had no idea what was next. My scholarship was coming to an end. I had missed out on the kind of endorsements needed to go pro. Suddenly it felt like my entire future was shaky and my dreams had been crushed.

My college coach stood with me. He didn't say anything, but I felt his steady presence.

Then, as he turned to walk off the field, over his shoulder he called out, "I'll see you at practice on Monday."

It was a statement, but it could have been a question, because neither of us knew if I would show up.

I did.

We acted like nothing happened. Like I hadn't lost, like I wasn't crushed, like I wasn't scared sh*tless about what my future held. We just went back to work.

But as the last weeks of the school year and track season were coming to an end, I was wrestling with disappointment and fear. The idea of going pro and working toward the 2008 Games with all the unknowns, financial and otherwise, felt like climbing Everest without any of the necessary resources needed to make the climb. I felt helpless and alone. I felt like I had failed, like I didn't have what it takes to become an Olympian, like the odds were stacked against me. But during those last weeks of my college season, while I was wrestling over what to do next, my coach was steady and unchanging.

Recently I asked him about those weeks after the trials, and he remembered a conversation that I didn't. He had told me that I was at a pivotal moment where I would have to take ownership of what I was capable of doing. He remembered saying something like "I'm not quitting. I'm not giving up on you. Are you?"

While I can't recall this conversation, it sounds like something he'd say. And it's always been true. His strength and belief in me have often been a source of encouragement when I didn't know if I was good enough or if I could keep going.

My coach, Dennis Shaver, is a man of few words. He is measured and loyal, and for more than twenty years we have shared an intense honesty. I trust him with my life. And that's a big deal, something he began earning from the first day I met him.

LSU

During my senior year at Roosevelt High School, I got recruiting letters from all over the United States.

As a high school senior, I wasn't dreaming about the Olympics; I was looking to get out of my circumstances. No one in my family had ever gone to college. I knew this was an opportunity to break the cycle of poverty. I knew that a college education would help me change my life. So a scholarship was a big deal and my main focus. And track and field was just a means to that end.

At the time, I believed that was absolutely true. But in hindsight, I know I loved the sport.

I started going on college visits. I knew I wanted to go to the Southeastern Conference (SEC). My mom's side of the family lives in Texas, including my grandparents and a lot of my aunts and uncles. I felt like if I needed to get away and still have my family see me compete, I needed to be at a school in the SEC so I would be close enough for them to come to the meets.

Since I lived in Iowa, I visited Iowa State, but not on an official recruiting trip. I drove up and they gave me a one-day tour. Iowa State is a good school and I love Iowa, but they were just not competitive enough in track and field. So it was never really an option for me.

I am actually pretty smart; I was on the academic honor roll in high school. I'm competitive too. "If you're going to do something, you should win at it." That's how the saying goes, right? So my track coach wanted me to visit at least one school known for outstanding academics. My first recruiting trip was to Vanderbilt in Nashville, Tennessee. Academically it is an amazing school. But when I looked at their record wall, I discovered I had already beaten all their records as a high school senior.

After Vanderbilt was the University of South Carolina in Columbia. I really connected with the athletes I met there; several are still good friends of mine. I was treated well and it was a beautiful campus, but they didn't have a solid indoor track and their program was not established. As of this writing, I think they have won nationals only once. It was also the farthest from my mother's family in Texas.

Then there was the University of Tennessee in Knoxville. I loved Tennessee because they had a great women's basketball team that was winning titles and championships. It was clear they supported women's sports. I liked the campus, and they had a decent track and field program. Plus, they had all four seasons, something that intrigued me, an Iowa girl.

The University of Georgia was probably the only school I wasn't really feeling. Partly because when I got there, they put me in a dorm with someone. While all the other colleges were rolling out the red carpet, putting me up in hotels and basically wining and dining me— without the wine because I was eighteen—Georgia seemed to think it would be cool if I experienced the dorm life.

I was like, "All right, I see what you're doing here. But I've lived most of my life in small apartments with five people. I already know the dorm life." When I told them I wasn't interested in a dorm room, they put me in a hotel. I don't remember much else about Georgia.

Did I mention I was only eighteen? Did I mention I was alone on these trips? Did I mention I wasn't living with Mom and Dad but with foster parents who weren't talking it through with me, that I wasn't particularly close to any of my coaches, that I didn't have a best friend or confidant to help me with the most important decision of my entire life at that point?

That's a hard challenge as a high school senior. While most seniors are just trying to figure out where to go academically, I was trying to figure out an athletic career as well.

Okay, so maybe I wasn't dreaming of the Olympics yet, but neither was I dreaming of being second best. I have always wanted to compete to win, and winning means more when it's done against the best.

Then there was Louisiana State University in Baton Rouge. It arguably has the best track and field program in the nation. And they have an incredible legacy in track. At that point they had won thirteen national titles.

In a row!

That was insane.

To put it into perspective, the New England Patriots have won only eleven straight AFC Eastern Division titles and only one back-to-back Super Bowls. Yes, only.

Or maybe you are a Duke Blue Devils basketball fan and think they are a dominant program with five NCAA titles. They're not even close to what LSU's track and field program has accomplished.

Here's my point: you would need to combine the unbroken records of both the Patriots and the Blue Devils to begin to grasp the dominance of LSU's track and field program. So LSU very much intrigued me.

On my recruiting trip to LSU, I roomed with Muna Lee, who was probably one of the top recruits to come out of high school. She was the best US sprinter at the time and went on to become an Olympic athlete. And then there was Stephanie Durst, another recruit who would become an all-American sprinter and go pro for several years after LSU. So I was with some really heavy hitters for high school athletes. That also left an impression.

After the recruiting season, I had to make the decision.

My high school made a big deal about what school I would choose, holding a press conference when I signed. Even up to the last minute, I was going back and forth between LSU and South Carolina. At the press conference I had both letters of intent.

I chose LSU.

Sometimes it takes hindsight to see how God works. I truly believe God played a role in that decision, and I am so thankful He has the final word in my life. LSU is where I found my coach, and some twenty years later, I still train there, which is highly unusual. It's been a good home base.

It's not that I prayed about it. At that point, I was a baby in my faith. But you can't convince me God wasn't guiding my decision.

God and a man named Dennis Shaver.

RECRUITED BY THE BEST

What truly tipped the scales in LSU's favor was Coach Shaver, who was their assistant coach at the time.

After all the visits came the recruiting phone calls. Each college got one recruiting call with me per week. I don't know what the NCAA rules are now, but back then they just talked my head off. Each coach tried to keep me on the phone as long as possible to really capitalize on the call.

For about four months, coaches were calling me and talking and talking and talking. But I was a quiet high school girl. Talking to people I didn't really know for hours at a time wasn't something I enjoyed. I mean, what sprinter wants to talk for hours? A sprinter's job is to get a lot done in the least amount of time.

And then there was Coach Shaver. His calls were four minutes. He didn't waste time. He got down to business. The calls were so short that I almost thought he didn't want me to come to LSU.

It left an impression.

It's kind of like if you're dating and all these guys are calling you and wooing you and talking about themselves nonstop, but then there's one guy who's playing hard to get.

I chose that guy.

Because, well, *challenge accepted*.

This was the beginning of what has become one of the most important relationships in my life and career.

CHALLENGE ACCEPTED

I wasn't the only one who accepted a challenge. When Coach Shaver decided to coach me, well, he accepted one too. You know, some athletes are easy to coach and others are pretty demanding. I'm one of those demanding athletes.

In my freshman year, our team was at USC for an NCAA track meet. There was a tailwind of forty to fifty miles an hour. In a sport like hurdling, where winning and losing are defined by hundredths of a second, where national and world records are made in less than the blink of an eye, the weather—in particular, the wind—is measured and recorded because it plays a significant role.

A tailwind is when you are pushed by the wind. You might think this is helpful, but for hurdlers, it's a problem. It can actually be too much assistance, and it can throw you off.

But I was too young to know the power of wind. This was my first year at LSU, and all I wanted to do was prove myself, to compete and win—wind, rain, or shine. Like in *Rocky IV*, line me up in a Russian snowstorm and I'd kick its butt.

I don't remember that Coach Shaver was concerned about the wind, or that the officials had considered postponing the track meet. I just remember lining up and then exploding off the blocks into disaster. Runners were hitting hurdles and falling all around me.

And then the unthinkable happened.

I hit a hurdle.

And fell.

It was the first time in my life I fell in a competition. Middle school, high school, I never hit a hurdle; I never fell. To be clear, that's quite rare. When most hurdlers are starting out, they fall all the time. But not me.

And not only did I fall; I fell twice! So, yeah, I ran, hit a hurdle, and fell. Then I got up, ran, hit another hurdle, and fell again. Two times in one race.

I took skin off my arm, hip, and knee. I was shocked and pissed; not because of torn skin but because I fell. I was embarrassed, maybe even ashamed, and it came out as anger.

Apparently I was, as Coach Shaver refers to it, "a little fired up."

Apparently, as Coach Shaver likes to tell it, I showed my frustration to everyone around me. And apparently everybody was "catching it," from my head coach to the trainers to my teammates to, you know, the bus driver.

I don't remember how fired up I was. But I suppose I could have been a little short with those around me, and maybe the bus driver too.

The way I remember it, I just wanted to run again after I'd fallen, but no one, especially my head coach, seemed to be willing to let that happen.

I told my coaches, "Put me in the 400-meter hurdles."

Who cares that I hadn't trained in the 400 meter, that it wasn't an event I ran in. All I wanted was a chance to redeem myself. Even now that seems perfectly understandable, yet none of my coaches would allow it, and no one seemed to understand.

So maybe I got a little fired up.

At the bus driver.

Oh, okay. I see it now.

Yeah, I can be a little fiery sometimes, maybe a lot fiery. Some of it is personality, and it has served me well in my professional career. But some of my demanding anger that day had to do with the pressure I felt during my first year at college.

I was alone in the world and felt the pressure to prove I could overcome my impoverished and broken childhood, prove I could compete with the best, prove I belonged there. Looking back, I now understand that I had wrapped my identity and future into every hurdle I cleared during those early years. So when I fell, it wasn't just a lost race; it was my entire life—past, present, and future—that felt uncertain.

Most of my teammates and coaches perceived my outburst as

overreacting, but Coach Shaver was able to see past my fire. He was able to see me for who I truly was and who I could truly become.

On the bus ride home, while I nursed my wounds and privately contemplated leaving LSU for another school, my head coach was privately arguing the same idea with Coach Shaver. I didn't know it at the time, but there was a serious discussion about whether they would keep "this girl on the team."

I've since learned how Coach Shaver leveraged his trust with the head coach to argue for keeping me on. "Coach, we need to rethink this. You know she's a passionate person," he said. It's true—and very generous, 'cause apparently, you know, I yelled at the bus driver too.

Coach Shaver has had my back from the beginning, but it wasn't like he told me about it. Nor could he. That's not how trust is earned. That's what he was doing and has always done, building trust. And that takes time.

Slowly, while fighting every day for my hurdling life, I discovered I could trust Coach Shaver. And as he steadily earned my trust, much of my competitive world steadied as well.

TALENT AND COMMITMENT

When I got to LSU, there was so much tailwind in my life that I felt like every day, at any moment, I would crash and burn. I felt pressure just to make it through a day, let alone graduate. My future was always hanging in the balance as I struggled to break free from the broken parts of my past, from poverty, while trying to prove to myself I belonged. It was tough.

I suddenly found myself at LSU both motivated and insecure. I got the impression Coach Shaver wasn't 100 percent sure about me, which I now know was true. I had to earn his trust as well. I hadn't originally been on LSU's radar until a former LSU hurdler who had gone to my high school four years earlier had recommended me to Coach Shaver.

I also now know that it was not my talent alone that convinced Coach Shaver to offer me a scholarship; it was what he refers to as "my commitment." As I've heard him say, "Talent alone doesn't make a good hurdler; it's talent *and* commitment." Somehow our four-minute conversations convinced Coach Shaver to further investigate whether I was committed. When I first arrived at LSU, neither of us truly knew how I was going to do.

I was dedicated and driven, but I was also very raw. I was struggling at practices. Many times, after running, the other athletes would walk off the track while I'd have to go find a place to throw up. I was throwing up all the time. The workouts were just so hard, especially since the humidity in Louisiana was unfamiliar and suffocating. It was so hard to breathe. It was like trying to run in a sauna.

On top of that, I was having a hard time adjusting to being on the team. I wasn't really vibing with some of my teammates.

But what was most difficult and caused me to feel insecure was that I wasn't the only freshman hurdler. I knew LSU would have a senior hurdler, but Coach Shaver had recruited two other freshmen hurdlers who were also really good. So every day we were all fighting for our spots. I didn't know about everyone's scholarship situation, but I was convinced there was no way he was going to keep all of us on scholarship for four years.

It was an intimidating situation to go to the best school in the country for track and then have to battle it out with two other freshmen and a senior. You know, if the senior beats you, it's okay because she is a senior. (Not that she did, because in my first race against her, I won.) But when you're on day one in practice and you are battling with two other freshmen hurdlers, yeah, that's gonna intensify the situation really quickly.

So every day, while practicing, the insecurity I had felt from those four-minute phone calls was reaffirmed. *Maybe they didn't want me here or weren't that confident in me. Did I make a mistake? Can I do this?* These thoughts plagued my days and nights.

Added to that, I knew the head coach wasn't a big fan. We didn't get along. My blowup with him the day I fell? It wasn't the first.

That's why on that bus ride back, and for most of my first year, I considered transferring to another school. Between the friction with my head coach, the competition with my teammates, and the workouts, I was dying.

But I didn't quit. That's one thing I learned about myself that first year at LSU. I don't quit. Even if competing nearly breaks me, I don't quit.

That drive was my way of earning Coach Shaver's respect and trust. I was committed.

And over that year, I learned that my coach was committed as well.

It didn't happen in some epic moment. It wasn't some great act from Coach Shaver that made me trust him. It was his consistency. His day-in-day-out calm, fair, unruffled, wise approach began to settle me.

His steady, unchanging confidence won me over.

I had been living such a shaky existence for so long, working to prove myself, to get out of poverty, there were few I could trust. It was a scary, topsy-turvy world I lived in, and I felt alone.

Then Coach Shaver earned my trust.

COACH SHAVER

Coach Shaver has coached me for twenty years now. We have seen a lot together.

He is one of the most quietly confident men I know. He and I are actually similar, although not in the quiet department, because I can be loud and fiery while Coach Shaver is more reserved. But we both have an intense confidence in our abilities.

I have been asked if he is a humble man. That's funny. The answer is no, absolutely not. At least not when it comes to his belief in himself. But he is a humble man when it comes to finding the best way to work with an athlete. He is patient and kind and calm, and powerfully so. Nothing seems to faze him, which provides stability and confidence when I need it most, because, you know, sometimes I get "a little fired up." That's a nice way to describe me, but it might give the wrong impression that Coach lets me walk all over him. He doesn't. Not even a little.

One time, at my third Olympic trials, I felt like there was no way I was gonna make the team. I was losing my focus on the track, and I was getting very escalated. My arms were probably flailing, because that's what happens when I'm overwhelmed. I may not have been screaming, but . . . who am I kidding, I was screaming. I got so intense and in his face, and he just walked away.

So when I say patient, kind, and calm, I don't mean soft. He's no Mister Rogers. There is a sternness to him. He doesn't get intimidated, and that can be quite intimidating. He is always calm, but it's the kind of calm that is more powerful than the storm. It both reassures and motivates, which is what I need, especially when I am in the heart of a storm.

I think Coach Shaver is a big reason why I am still in the game. And not just because he has been a good coach, stable and steady.

He's also brutally honest. He can deliver bad news in a way that doesn't discourage but allows me to find the 1 percent chance to fix something.

He can break down a bad race between rounds at a championship and give me fewer than six words that can change my whole outlook. So many times he has helped turn potentially bad races into good races simply with one cue. It reminds me of when I'm having an awful day and I read the Bible and find one psalm or proverb that completely changes my outlook.

Coach Shaver is always in my corner; that's a big deal. When I got to college, I had nowhere I could put my trust. There was no home I could return to, no one I could count on to bail me out if I were in a bind.

My dad loves me, but I couldn't count on him when I was in trouble. I know many people who wonder if their dads love them, but that has never been something I've had to wrestle with about my dad. We've never had a four-minute conversation; we talk for hours. But when it comes to dads, availability is the most important, and mine often wasn't there.

Coach Shaver has always been there. He is the positive, consistent male role model in my life. He can be counted on; I can access his calmness and wisdom when I need it. He is stable, the type of person I can go to when there are twenty different problems in my brain. I can dump them all on him, and he's gonna give me one sentence of clarity, the one thing I need to do. I know if the proverbial stuff hits the fan, he's got my back.

LSU is where I learned confidence, and where I began to become a good hurdler because of Coach Shaver. Coaches can tell you a hundred things you are doing wrong, but only because they are partnered with you on the one thing they believe you can do right, maybe even better than anyone else.

Good coaches believe in you so you can believe in yourself. They help you discover who you are and what you're on the planet to do. When you can place your trust in a trustworthy person, you begin to feel a sense of security. In that context, I became more confident.

I think we all need a champion, someone who believes in us and can give us wisdom along the way. My dad gave me street smarts, often illegal, but they taught me the wisdom of survival. Coach Shaver gave me wisdom on how to get stronger and better. And God gives me wisdom that surpasses all human understanding; He gives me faith.

I am growing in my faith. I continue to learn how to trust God. And it has been life-giving. I'm also continuing to learn how to trust others from people God has put in my life, chief among them Coach Shaver.

I came to LSU in 2000, and Coach Shaver has been in my life ever since. He has been a consistent source of wisdom and coaching, and he has earned my trust. Trust can be earned only by a trustworthy person.

Above all, God continues to prove trustworthy. My faith in God has sustained me in the dark days, and it has empowered me to believe again when I have experienced pain, disappointment, and loss.

I think my faith is maybe the most important thing for trying again, for attacking the next hurdle.

FIVE

A BIRACIAL GIRL IN A BLACK AND WHITE WORLD

Growing up, I didn't like seafood. I was a midwestern, landlocked Iowa girl. You may not know this, but Iowa ranks second nationally in red meat production. Not that I grew up on red meat. Most of my protein came from beans; they were more affordable. But one thing that was never on the home menu was seafood.

The handful of times I did have seafood before living in Louisiana was at Red Lobster. And while we can all agree that their cheddar biscuits are from God above, if you ever want to insult Cajuns, tell them you love seafood and then follow that up with your favorite Red Lobster dish. In Louisiana, Red Lobster is a curse word.

And then there's the crawfish boil. A crawfish boil (pronounced "boll") is a cultural initiation. If you haven't been to one, you can't call yourself a southerner.

In the South there are plenty of debates about the best way to cook crawfish, but there is no debating the best way to eat them: rip off the tail and suck all the flavor from the head. Personally, I love the whole thing: head, tail, arms, legs, whatever you gotta do to get to the spices.

I'm like Bobby Boucher, the Adam Sandler character in *The Waterboy*. I can kill a pound of them quick. Which is how you are supposed to eat them, because crawfish refrigerate about as well as a Happy Meal. The repercussions of eating them later are much worse. I write from experience. You don't save crawfish. You just don't do that.

When it came to seafood, adjusting to the South was fairly easy, but nothing else was.

Yes, I had my coach, but during the time it took to know and trust him, I had a world of adjustments that nearly derailed my freshman year and could have killed my career.

I was overwhelmed by the physical toll of LSU's track and field program; I was barely surviving the workouts. I was also going to classes, including study hall because all athletes had mandatory study halls, and then I had papers and tests and more classes. I was exhausted.

And yet all these things were expected. I mean, I knew how to compete; I was born for it. I knew how to be disciplined in my academic life, I knew how to remain focused, and I knew I wouldn't quit. But there was a new challenge I had no experience with, and it had to do with some of my teammates.

I wasn't really able to vibe with them. I'd even had a few fights.

When you are in such an intense, competitive pressure cooker, it's not unusual to have heated interactions. But you get over it and you move on. However, this disconnect wasn't just on the track or in class; it was deeper, and it was cultural.

While adjusting to the Cajun spelling of the word *go—geaux*, really—and learning to love seafood were less burdensome, the cultural differences actually touched on who I was as a human being.

MIXED

There is a pro track and field race in Iowa called the Drake Relays. Iowa is where I am from, so when my pro athlete friends go to compete in this race, they're comfortable asking, "Where are all the black people?"

Growing up I didn't realize there were so few black people in Iowa. It wasn't until I moved to Louisiana that I understood how predominantly white Iowa is. It's not that black people don't live there—I had several black friends and teammates—but there are certain parts of my home state where you can go for days without seeing a black person. That's not the case in the South.

I am mixed. Mom is white, and Dad is black and Native American. So half my family is white and the other half is black. *Family*, I think, is an important word to grab ahold of as we continue. When it comes to race issues, the clashing we see on the news, the combative viewpoints, the politically charged antagonistic approaches, they all have to be worked out if you are in a mixed family. You see, there are no one-sided perspectives, no black or white—pun intended—viewpoints in the house of a biracial person.

But in Louisiana, I was suddenly thrust into a very black and white world.

Looking back, I was admittedly less familiar with my black heritage. While racism was certainly something I had experienced growing up, I had a white mom and lived in the North, so it hadn't impacted me the same way it impacted my new black teammates.

There were a lot of different black roots on the team; some were from Jamaica, Grenada, and other countries with a predominately black population.

In Louisiana, I was plunged into the epicenter of centuries-long atrocities, where the cultural divide was deep and the lines between black and white were seemingly immovable. I was getting an experiential education about the cultural realities of being black in the South. But I was only half black; the other half of me was white. And there didn't seem to be any room for me to be both—at least that's how it felt. Basically, I felt like I had to deny my mother for the sake of my father, or the other way around.

I remember sitting on the team bus with a girl from Jamaica, and she asked me about my parents. I told her I was mixed.

In her Jamaican accent, she said, "Nah, gurl, you are black."

I repeated, "No, I am mixed."

She then argued with me, mad that I wouldn't identify as just black.

That wasn't the first time I'd had that argument. In grade school I remember people getting mad that I didn't identify as full black. I told my mom about one such argument, and she said, "You tell them I carried you for nine months and that half of my blood is running in your veins. So to deny being mixed is to deny me."

In the South, I felt like I could be either black or white but not both. And I didn't know how to handle it. I felt lost and defensive, mostly for not being black enough because that was where I experienced the greatest pressure.

I know that seems strange, because in the world we live in today, it's almost always the other way around. But in my life, I have felt racism from both white and black people. And I am not writing about systemic racism here. I am writing about individual racism, that ugly sense of superiority based on race. I know it's not a popular belief, but I believe individual racism is something anyone can be guilty of.

As a mixed person living in a racially divided America today, I often feel like I am not white enough for white people or black enough for black people. Just like when I was younger, people still want me to draw lines. It's astounding how often someone demands that I choose a side and deny a part of myself on behalf of another part of myself.

Here are a couple of social media comments that represent hundreds more just like them:

> **Stranger on Twitter:** President Obama is bi-racial but
> identifies as black. Alicia Keys is bi-racial and identifies
> as black, same with Halle Berry and [Mariah Carey].
> **Me:** [That's] good for them, [but it's] not my journey.

> **Stranger on Twitter:** Apologize to your own people.
> **Me:** I'm biracial.

In a country that seems determined to define the line between white and black, I find myself in the middle. To draw lines is to literally deny a part of myself and divide my family. So, from my experience, which is all I have, racism is not just a white problem; it's a human problem.

Before you cancel me, hear me out.

SYSTEMIC RACISM

I know there is systemic racism toward black people. I have experienced it.

I've had a cop demand to see my ID in my own house. He talked down to me like I was a piece of trash. Black trash. In my own house! He didn't believe it was my property and demanded that I prove I owned the place. That police officer didn't see me as a woman, a college graduate, a professional athlete, or even an Olympian. He saw a black person.

I know from experience that there are bad cops who give leniency to white people but not to black people. I've been pulled over and felt the racial hostility. I've been in the car when Mom—a blue-eyed blonde white woman—has been pulled over, and the experience was different for her.

When black people talk about having to de-escalate the police, I understand. I've had to do it myself. And no one should ever have to do that.

But before I continue, I have to share that I've had more positive interactions with police and public servants than negative. The fact is, I believe the majority of our public servants are good people who are doing their best.

While the majority of Americans aren't racist, I know systemic racism is real. I know there is a wealth disparity between blacks and whites. All I have to do is look at those on the black side of my family who work as hard as the white side of my family. They have to hurdle so much more just to keep their heads above water in a world that economically favors a lighter skin color.

So there's a problem.

But how do I, Lolo Jones, address it?

That was the question I was asking myself when a black man by the name of George Floyd was brutally killed by a white policeman and the whole world burned with the injustice of it.

I was furious. I wanted to do something. I wanted to add my voice to the outrage. I wanted to address such horrific abuses of power. So I took a month off from social media.

Counterintuitive? Maybe.

But I can be a little too honest about my feelings on social media, and I wanted to be helpful. So why take a month off? It would have been easy to post "Black Lives Matter" because, obviously, they do. But remember that word *family*, which is the lens through which I always want to have this conversation. I think it is the only way forward.

I wanted to think through not just what I would post but also what I could do after; not just my reaction but my response. Essentially, I wanted to be clear about what actions I would put behind my words.

I was angry, but I wanted to direct my anger in a way that would help people—black people, white people, all people, no matter their skin color—because I am mixed, because there are no lines for me, because I believe the only way forward is together.

Because family.

When I was clearheaded, I posted an old Polaroid image of my dad dressed in his white prison jumpsuit taken during a visit from my mom. I wrote,

This is my mom visiting my dad in prison.

My dad is 87 years old. He was born in 1933, fought in the Korean War, and when he returned, he suffered systemic racism.

He spent half his life in prison. He was Black in America. He lived during segregation, during the 50s and 60s.

But against it all [. . .]

I'm the product of these two. Fighting through it all. When interracial dating was frowned upon they chose to show [how to move forward]:

We gotta do this together. Unity.[1]

THE GOOD SAMARITAN

In Luke 10, a Jewish leader, "an expert in the law" (v. 25), approached Jesus and asked about eternal life. During their discussion, they agreed that everything in the law and in relationships boils down to "'Love the Lord your God with all your heart and with all your soul and with all your strength and with all your mind'; and, 'Love your neighbor as yourself'" (v. 27).

Then the Jewish leader, who wanted to justify himself, asked Jesus, "And who is my neighbor?" (v. 29).

In response, Jesus told a story that captured my imagination as a child and still guides me today. It's a story called the Good Samaritan. It went like this . . .

A man was traveling between cities when robbers attacked him. They stripped him of his clothing, beat him within an inch of his life, and left him on the roadside.

Then a priest came across the beaten, bloodied man. But he didn't stop to help; instead, he continued on his way. Next, a Levite came across the beaten man. He also ignored the man and continued on his way. Finally, a Samaritan came across the helpless, wounded man. The Samaritan stopped, bandaged his wounds, put him on his donkey, and carried him to a nearby inn where he paid the innkeeper to look after the man until he fully recovered.

When Jesus finished telling this story, He asked the Jewish leader, "Which of these three do you think was a neighbor to the man who fell into the hands of robbers?" (v. 36).

The law expert replied, "The one who had mercy on him."

Then Jesus said to him, "Go and do likewise" (v. 37).

I loved this story as a child because of how simple it is to see what is right and what is wrong, and how a kind act can change a person's life. As I got older, I loved this story because I understood the context of Jesus' words and suddenly realized what a rebel He was.

At the time Jesus told this story, Jews despised Samaritans and treated them very poorly. They were seen as racially and religiously inferior. So in this story, Jesus was not just revealing the kind heart of God; He was addressing inequality and how to deal with it.

Go and do likewise.

There is so much we can learn from those words.

AFTER WE MARCH

What are we doing after we post on social media? What are we doing after we march? What are we doing with our outrage? Because, you know, anger alone doesn't fix anything.

Anger over injustice is the right emotion to feel. I think marching is a good response, since it can bring awareness to an issue, which is important. But when anger goes unchecked or doesn't have a clear, unifying objective, marches turn violent. And that helps no one. In my opinion, if a person's anger doesn't translate into actions that actually help those who are experiencing inequality, it's pretty much pointless and often counterproductive.

I imagine the Good Samaritan was angry at the injustice committed against the beaten man; it would be a natural emotional response to injustice. But then the Samaritan helped right a wrong through acts of kindness and generosity.

I have worked in the inner city, and I've volunteered in some of the poorest churches where kids go to after-school programs to get free meals, because otherwise they're not going to get dinner. And you know what? There aren't that many volunteers.

For me, it's frustrating to see so many people post about Black Lives Matter and then leave their couches only to protest. If black lives really matter, then, okay, protest, but there's a whole inner city of kids where you live who need help. So maybe after you protest, after you march, go do something that helps someone who has fewer opportunities than you do.

To be clear, I am not trying to distract from the fact that there is systemic racism and that it needs to be highlighted and addressed. But for me, after posting about it on my social media platforms, after marching, I want to be doing something about it. I want to help.

For me, this isn't just about being black or white; this is about what it means to be a Christian. And Jesus tells us what it looks like to be a Christian: love the Lord your God with all your heart, soul, mind, and strength, and then love your neighbor as you love yourself.

Love isn't just a social media post or chanting "Black lives matter" at a march; love is action. It has to be an action.

What does being a good neighbor look like? In the biblical story of the Good Samaritan, Jesus said it looks like one person meeting the needs of another person. To me the issue of race is as simple as loving God with all our hearts, souls, minds, and strength, and then loving our neighbors—our black neighbors, our white neighbors, our biracial neighbors, all our neighbors—as we love ourselves. It's about family.

What if everyone in America, regardless of skin color, volunteered with their churches or nonprofits to feed, clothe, and care for the poorest and most oppressed among us? I truly think this would have an exponentially greater impact than just marching. It most certainly would accomplish more than violent or destructive acts. Where is the willingness to do something? Because things change when people—all people—are humble enough to do something kind and generous for their neighbors.

As a Christian I believe our actions reveal the love of God for our fellow humans. So I'm fine with posting a blacked-out image on Instagram. I'm all about getting on social media to make a statement. And I'm all for marching. But after that, let's do something that really helps people!

CHECK YOUR PRIVILEGE

I think white privilege is a thing, and I think there's some serious soul-searching that needs to go on in my white American "family." But white privilege is not the only privilege. I think almost everyone has some form of privilege; it's not just about race.

I also think it's important to see your privilege. It helps a person live authentically and humbly.

I have friends, black and white, who were more privileged than I was simply because they grew up with two parents in the home the whole time. I have friends, white and black, who grew up more privileged because they had money, and so they had more opportunities than I did.

Yes, we can point to white privilege. But we can also point to American privilege, historic privilege, gender privilege, and many other kinds of privilege.

Did you know that the Olympic Games was originally only for male athletes? The modern Olympics started in 1896, and at that time only men could compete.

Amazingly, as early as 1900, women were able to enter the Games, but only in sports that were "compatible with their femininity and fragility."[2] Seriously, *fragility*. I don't know what these men were talking about. Have you ever seen my face when I hurdle? There's nothing fragile about it.

It wasn't until 1922 that women could compete in the 100-meter hurdles at the Women's World Games. In 1932, it was truncated to the 80-meter hurdles at the Olympic Games. And not until the 1972 Olympics was the distance increased to 100 meter.[3] My point: I am privileged to compete in the 100-meter hurdles simply because of when I was born. Thirty-five years earlier I would have been considered too fragile.

I think recognizing privilege is a healthy thing to do regardless of race or gender. It gives us access to empathy, and our nation could use that right now. Most of us have some form of privilege we can be thankful for. I also think when we are able to recognize our own privilege, we can begin to recognize inequality without feeling threatened. And maybe then, we can live more generously toward those around us.

You see, while I understand that BLM is a political movement, the fact is, black lives matter. And when black people hear someone say, "All lives matter," it feels like that person is intentionally denying inequality exists. So check your privilege. Black lives matter.

I also understand that while protests can bring awareness and potentially lead to new laws, they alone don't change our neighborhoods. And destruction and violence are just stupid; they help no one. Instead, go help those who are experiencing greater inequality than you are. There are so many ways to help your underprivileged neighbors.

Personally, I think more can be done to protest systemic racism through serving hungry kids than through marching. I am not against marching. I just think racial justice and reconciliation are advanced exponentially when we all start acting like the Good Samaritan.

CREATED EQUAL

I was born into a biracial family. I grew up poor. I was raised in a broken family with a father who was incarcerated for much of my life. At times I even participated in petty crimes to survive.

The statistics all say I shouldn't have experienced success. But I have. And there are a lot of reasons for this, many I have already noted. I had a family that did their best, a church, a competitive mindset, coaches and others who've helped me along the way. But another reason is that I was given opportunity, and once again, I worked it. I didn't quit.

I have experienced racism too. I have been called the N-word. That's part of my story, but it's not the whole story. I've also been given opportunities because I live in America where, though we still have injustice and inequality, we also have opportunity.

That's a real thing.

In the US Declaration of Independence, there is a line that says, "All men are created equal."

Yeah, I know that when it was written, the white men who wrote it didn't consider black people as equals. The same goes for Native American people, Latinx people, Asian people, and even women. I am also aware that several who signed it actually owned slaves.

But none of that changes the truth of the statement, or the fact that so many in the United States continue to champion that foundational principle. It's an ideal that good people in our nation fight for even today.

While it certainly was hypocritical and disgusting that slavery existed even while this document was being written, the ideals of freedom are in the very DNA of our country. I know that's not popular to write about these days. But those ideals, for me, are bigger than words written in our Declaration of Independence; they are truths Jesus revealed on the cross. Those ideals are interwoven in my faith.

Jesus revealed God's great love for all humanity and taught equality at a time when there was far less freedom than there is now. Jesus taught us to love our neighbor, even our Samaritan neighbor. So, "all men [and women, of all skin colors,] are created equal" is the truth. And it's a big deal for me.

It's my desire that we push toward equality in this country and around the world. And even though I have experienced inequality in my life, because I grew up in America where "liberty and justice for all" is still very much the pursuit of good people, I had opportunities to work hard and break through.

A FINAL THOUGHT

That first year in college was hard, but I didn't quit. Over time I began to build friendships. I got pretty close with Stephanie Durst and Muna Lee. We're still close.

I'm telling you it didn't start out that way. I fought with Muna and Stephanie all the time in college. I fought so badly with Stephanie one time that it became physical. Coach Shaver had a meeting with us and told us, "One day you guys are going to be best friends. And years from now, you guys are going to still know what each other is doing."

He was right. After college, Steph and I became best friends. We ran pro track races all over Europe together, and even though she retired years ago, we have stayed connected.

Any cultural differences between us have become opportunities to understand each other. And we had more in common than differences. Most of all, we were focused; we wanted to go pro.

We weren't your typical college students either. We weren't partiers. It's not that we were *trying* to be good girls; we were just good girls who were athletes, too focused on track to do anything else. There was no time to party or to do the college things that most movies portray. No time to join a sorority or some club. No time to participate in extracurricular activities. And no time to dwell on our past experiences with inequality. We were too tired from the workouts.

There was no free time. Well, maybe a little free time. Because for a minute, I had a boyfriend. He was on the basketball team. He was a solid Christian. And he was black.

He shared my commitment to wait until marriage to have sex. And he definitely helped with my faith because he was a strong Christian. His family was really strong in their faith as well. This relationship helped me to culturally adjust in Louisiana and to grow in my faith.

Then there was my boyfriend's church.

In the South, everyone goes to church. It was one aspect of the culture that helped me. And my boyfriend's church was definitely different from many of the churches I knew in the Midwest.

I remember being shocked at the worship, the people, the sense of life and freedom the first time I went to a service. It was Baptist, but not old Baptist. There were traditions, but it was very contemporary. People were clapping and swaying and speaking in tongues.

Where I'd come from, people might clap and possibly sway, but tongues was new to me.

It's not like they were dancing in the aisles; it wasn't that kind of church. But there was freedom and an expression of joy I hadn't experienced before. I met strong Christians who were really passionate about God.

It was the church, deep and wide, a family where black people, white people, and people of all races came together to worship God and love each other. There's that word *family* again.

Looking back, I realize it was probably more contemporary than most churches in the South at the time. But it was mixed, just like me. That church was a place where a biracial girl in a black and white world found a family of Good Samaritans. It was a new experience for a young person who, because of her youth, had thought she understood the whole race thing but had been struggling with the fact that she didn't have a clue.

I grew in my faith in that church. I grew in my hope for a world that doesn't see racial lines but instead can be a family.

In my mixed family, I learned how to find value in being black and white. And in my church family—where the people loved God, themselves, and all their neighbors regardless of race—I experienced the kind of unity this country needs. It was a game changer.

So maybe the love of God is the game changer regarding racial reconciliation.

While I don't pretend to have all the answers, I can tell my story and continue learning how to live with generosity and kindness toward my neighbors who don't have as many privileges as I do. And I can encourage others to love their neighbors—white and black and in between—as they love themselves.

Because the only way forward is together.

SIX

BREAKTHROUGH

You can watch a YouTube clip of my finals race, where I qualified for the Beijing Olympics, if you do a Google search for "Lolo Jones 2008 Olympic Trials."[1] It opens with an aerial shot of the oval track at Hayward Field stadium in Eugene, Oregon. Then you hear NBC Sports analyst Tom Hammond.

> **Tom Hammond:** Now to the final event for the Olympic trials with the last few chances to make the US team for Beijing. Up next will be the women's 100-meter hurdles. . . .

As color commentators Ato Boldon and Carol Lewis add additional observations, the camera cuts to a close-up of the 2004 Olympic gold medalist for the 100-meter hurdles, Joanna Hayes. Then the camera works its way down the line of runners and settles on me. I am bent over, focusing on my start.

Tom Hammond: Lolo Jones has been running well. Undefeated here in the rounds leading up to this final, and her 12.45 in the semifinals, fastest time of the world this year.

Ato Boldon: She has to be considered the favorite based on how she has looked. She was recalling the days when she would have to sit in Baton Rouge with no AC and wondering when could she quit her job. Should she make this team, it would be a very good time. She is 100 meters away.

The camera cuts away from me to a second camera behind the blocks, which captures four of my seven competitors and then, just past them, the stands full of spectators. It's a bright, sunny day, with a slight tailwind. It's perfect race weather.

Hammond and his colleagues continue to comment on my competition, particularly Damu Cherry, Dawn Harper, and Joanna Hayes. Over the commentators' banter, I can hear the announcer say through the megaphone-quality stadium speakers, "On your mark."

The camera cuts again, now focusing down the starting line as each runner fits her feet into the blocks, back left, then front right. Each runner's right knee settles into the track, the other knee raised. Then each runner positions her hands, first the left, then the right, just behind the starting line.

I am in lane four, and one of the last to settle in as the analysts continue to comment on my competitors. But their voices become quieter, almost a whisper, as thousands of spectators suddenly get quiet.

The camera cuts one last time to Joanna Hayes as she resets, before finally cutting to a wide-angle shot that shows all the runners.

Then, through the crackling speakers, we hear one word: "Set."

As one, knees lift and hips rise as we move to set position; backs flat, heads up and aligned. For a heartbeat you can hear a pin drop. Then the sound of the starting gun cracks, cutting through the silence.

Grunts and exhales are heard from the runners but they are quickly drowned out by thousands of cheering voices as we burst from the blocks.

Tom Hammond: It's a fair start!

The crowd is fully engaged by the time we clear the first hurdle, so it's hard to hear what Tom is saying after that. But a few phrases come through.

Tom Hammond: Lolo Jones gets away! . . . And now, it's
    Joanna Hayes and Damu Cherry . . . as they come for
    the final hurdle.

Twelve seconds is hardly long enough to describe what's happening, and by the time Tom finishes his statement, I've cleared nine hurdles.

Tom Hammond: Lolo Jones in command, with a dramatic win
    in the 100-meter hurdles!

I cross the finish line several paces ahead of everyone and the crowd is going crazy. I am celebrating with abandon, and the camera cuts to a close-up. I'm screaming, running, and jumping as I make fists with my hands. I can't contain my emotions.

Tom Hammond: It was close . . . but Lolo Jones! . . . She
proved to be the best in America!

Carol Lewis: You know, Tom, she has become a different
woman after that indoor [60-meter hurdles] world title.
She has been around for years but has never been able
to break through.

The camera is still close up on me, and I am still screaming in
elation.

Carol Lewis: When she won that world title, she said that
"My confidence was jumping leaps and bounds over
before," and she has been showing it each and every
race! She's strong and she's clean through the hurdles,
and that's what's so important.

Tom Hammond: Her time 12.29, wind aided, but such a
margin of victory here.

Ato Boldon: And remember, Tom, the world record in this
event was 12.21. That's been there for twenty years,
and here Lolo Jones comes and runs 12.29. One of the
fastest times ever, under all conditions.

I embrace the second- and third-place competitors, who are now
my Olympic teammates.

Tom Hammond: Damu Cherry second; Dawn Harper got
third.

I was going to the Olympics as the fastest hurdler in the world
that year!

Carol Lewis was correct when she said I had been around for years but had never been able to break through. For almost four years, I had been working. And now I had finally overcome. *Breakthrough!*

What I had done on the track was amazing. But that breakthrough race? It's even more amazing when viewed through the lens of what I had to overcome off the track in my first four years as a pro athlete.

GOING PRO

Professional track and field isn't like professional baseball or football. In those sports, if you excel in college and then go pro, you get a payday. If you sacrifice everything to be one of the best in college, you get financially rewarded.

Unfortunately, going pro in track and field is about so much more than hurdling. You could be the eighth-best hurdler in the world and still need to borrow a quarter at your local laundromat. In my first two years as a professional athlete after college, I actually lost money.

Can you spare a quarter?

Upon graduating, I found myself suddenly navigating agents, media, donors, and sponsorships—or the lack thereof. Then there were the endless financial pressures and limitations around training, travel, and recovery. Add to that the bills associated with life, like rent, water, and electricity, and I was broke. This is the typical story for most track and field athletes who try to go pro.

Here's how going pro works.

An average pro season for a hurdler is between twenty and thirty races, or meets, a year, starting in late winter through early spring with indoor 60-meter meets, and then continuing into the summer months with outdoor 100-meter meets. We compete all over the world for prize money that matches the different levels of competition. The higher the level of competition, the more we can earn. Early on in my career, I primarily competed in the lower-level races, where I could earn between $500 and $1,000 by placing first through third. (And if you don't place in the top three, you likely won't make anything.)

But wait, there's more!

A lot of people don't know that while a track meet organizer might supplement travel costs, most of the time, expenses fall on the athletes. This means that even if athletes place in the top three, they still have to subtract those costs.

So in some races, if I didn't place in the top three, I could actually lose money, which has happened.

For this reason, to compete professionally, I didn't just have to push myself physically, mentally, and emotionally; I also had to push myself financially. I had three jobs, and only one of them was as a professional athlete; the other two were at a Home Depot's Garden Center and a gym where, when I wasn't making smoothies, I was checking people in and cleaning gym equipment.

In those first two years as a pro, I had to cover travel, food, and sometimes even lodging for myself and my coach . . . all so I could compete for a chance to win enough money to cover travel, food, and lodging. Then I'd return to my jobs at Home Depot and the gym, and to the LSU track where I'd train in 95-degree weather, and then go home on my scooter to recover in a 105-degree apartment because I couldn't afford to turn on the air-conditioning.

Life was an exhausting balancing act of competing, working, and training, all so I could risk everything to be a professional track and field athlete.

I remember competing in a pro race in California and the next day making smoothies for people at the gym when the race, which was telecast a day later, came on the TV behind me. The people around me were like, "Wait, isn't that you?"

"Yeah, welcome to the life of a professional track and field athlete."

And I'm not done counting the expenses. On top of all the travel expenses, there are the training costs. Once you go pro, your coaches and trainers charge you. Using a school's facilities can also cost money, though LSU has been good to me. The most I've heard a college charging an Olympian is $20,000 per season just to use their track.

Then there is the rigorous physical schedule that puts wear and tear on your body and requires massages and chiropractic treatment. Most athletes get one or two massages a week because of the beating their bodies take. Add to that the possibility (and likelihood) of injury, which means doctors and surgery and physical therapy. It all costs money.

Why am I telling you all this? Well, first, because it's my story and I'm proud of how hard I've worked. But second, it's not just my story. American pro track and field athletes sacrifice so much for a chance to compete in a multibillion-dollar industry called the Olympic Games, which actually does very little to supplement the athletes in their preparation and pays nothing to those who compete in the Games.

I know a lot of Olympians and Olympic hopefuls who rack up $40,000 to $60,000 in credit card debt, because that's about how much it takes to properly train for the Olympics.

ABOUT THE OLYMPICS . . .

Give me a moment to get on my soapbox.

Most Olympians are ridiculously poor. This is primarily true around the world, but my focus is on American athletes and the US Olympic & Paralympic Committee (USOPC).

According to a 2012 income survey cited by *Forbes*, "Half of athletes ranked in the top 10 of their event in the U.S. earned less than $15,000 annually from all sources of income."[2] That includes endorsements, money won from competitions, corporate sponsors, and grants. Compared to your average worker, this isn't a lot.

You will often see Olympic athletes setting up fundraisers to pay for their parents' travel costs to the Olympic Games. Even though the Olympics is a multibillion-dollar industry, the athletes struggle to pay electric bills, work at minimum-wage jobs, and set up GoFundMe pages just to get their parents to the Games. Meanwhile, the International Olympic Committee (IOC), which calls its president and executives "volunteers," gives cash handouts (not salaries) in the realm of $250,000 annual allowance and $900 per diems, respectively.[3]

My friend, Peter Carlisle, who manages Olympic swimmer Michael Phelps and is managing director of the Olympic and Action Sports division at Octagon, helped me compile some data to highlight the financial disparity athletes face.

I know from experience that the only direct financial support Olympic athletes receive comes in the form of stipends, which are administered through the national governing body, such as the USA Track and Field or USA Bobsled (the "Athlete Performance-Support Training" on IRS Form 990), and Operation Gold Grant program. I've always felt that's a lazy way to do it, since the USOPC gives this support only *after* athletes actually achieve podium results in the competitions they need the funds to prepare for.

According to tax documents, between 2015 and 2019, the USOPC generated revenues of $1,177,936,959. (Yes, that's more than a billion dollars!) Yet it provided only $88,276,228 in direct funding to athletes, which is less than 8 percent of what the organization raised. In addition, the USOPC's average annual compensation for employees was $52,782,099, which is three times the average annual amount it put toward direct athlete funding. The USOPC also paid outside lawyers more than they paid athletes through the Operation Gold Grant program.[4]

A recent HBO documentary called *The Weight of Gold* highlights how the USOPC treats athletes like commodities, which negatively impacts our mental and emotional health. I recommend watching the film, but here are a few teaser quotes:

> "It's almost like a conveyor belt of athletes," said Gracie Gold, a figure skater who earned a bronze medal at the 2014 Winter Olympics. "You're doing really well, they keep you healthy, but like when you're off the conveyor belt, they have new athletes from every sport coming in."

> "When you're a younger athlete, they love you," I said. "You're the new fresh face. They want to promote you; they want to put you out there; they want everybody to fall in love with you. But after you've been to a few Olympics, you know, you just see, 'Oh, that's my replacement.' We got Sydney McLaughlin, nineteen years old, marketable, social media is on fire and, Lolo, that's your exit. Please [exit stage] right."

> Three-time Olympic speed skater Apolo Ohno said, "They are in the business of finding the latest and the greatest athletes, extracting the best performance out of them, and then going back to the trough to look for the latest and greatest athletes and doing it over and over, time and time again."[5]

The amount of pressure put on the athletes, especially with little to no access to financial support, is in a word, *wrong*; and in two words, *greedy exploitation*. The Olympics generates billions of dollars, and the athletes get nothing. Absolutely nothing. The gold medal isn't even solid gold; it's gold-plated.

And yet every athlete wants to win an Olympic gold medal, because the Olympics is the high–water mark for professional athletes, an opportunity to be the best in the world. As a professional athlete, I can say there is no greater honor than to be an Olympian.

The Games are rich in the tradition of promoting unity and diversity in a world in sore need of both. The hope and national pride that athletes have been able to inspire through the Games are amazing. So my soapbox thoughts aren't a diatribe against the Olympic Games. I simply want to be an advocate for the athlete who dreams, sacrifices, and works hard to reach the highest level of competition.

While I understand the nuanced and passionate viewpoints around athletes receiving payment, especially Olympic athletes, there has to be a way to support and compensate those who give everything to fulfill their dreams of representing their countries in the Games.

When an athlete can potentially make more by opting out of an Olympic team and instead choosing to compete in other international meets, there's something wrong with the system.

Of course, no athlete would even consider opting out of the Olympics; not only because it is the high–water mark for measuring the world's best but also because there *are* opportunities to get paid at the Olympics.

It's all about sponsorship.

Sponsorship is the financial lifeblood for a professional athlete. As difficult and frustrating as that fact is, for us to compete at the highest levels for any length of time, we have to find sponsors. Sponsorship is what most Olympic track and field athletes need to make it to the Games, and what they hope to further develop so they can continue in their careers.

It's why athletes sometimes get so crazed about attracting attention. The brighter the spotlight, the more sponsors they might secure.

SPONSORSHIPS AND TIPPING POINTS

In chapter 4, I wrote about the day in 2004 when I placed ninth and missed qualifying for the Olympic finals. Remember how devastated I was?

It wasn't just because I had missed out on the Olympics; it was also because I knew enough about the life of an unsponsored track and field athlete to understand that my hundredth-of-a-second loss meant my future in track had just gotten much harder, maybe even impossible.

Because I placed ninth, I was not offered a shoe contract, and I couldn't get in any race in Europe that offered prize money. It's crazy. The ninth-best NFL or NBA player has no financial worries, but the ninth-best American hurdler is basically unemployed.

Remember how Coach Shaver stood with me that day while I cried on the grass field next to the warm-up track? How he didn't say anything until he turned to walk away, and then said, "I'll see you at practice on Monday"? That Monday led to the next Monday and the next and to conversations with Coach Shaver that defined my Mondays for years to come.

"Lolo, this is a pivotal moment where you have to take ownership of what it is that you're capable of doing."

Those were hard words, but he wasn't wrong. If I was gonna get a second chance at making the Olympic team, I was going to have to do it with very little help from a sponsor.

Even though shortly after that conversation I was offered a deal from Nike, the amount—$7,500 a year for two years—was a joke, except they weren't joking and I wasn't laughing.

It was a crappy deal, but I took it. And, in Coach Shaver's words, "[took] ownership."

In my words, I went to work.

I knew how to work.

I knew how to break through.

I threw myself into my pro career with an obsession. I trained. I traveled and competed—Costa Rica one day, then on to the Philippines, Qatar, Japan, Spain, Norway, Canada, and Arkansas. I headed home to recover in my unair-conditioned apartment, because I still couldn't afford AC. And then I drove my scooter to my shift at Home Depot.

In 2005, I finished second in my first professional meet in Stuttgart, Germany.[6]

In my 2006 campaign, I ran even better. In July, I won the 100-meter hurdles at Heusden-Zolder, Belgium, clocking a personal best of 12.56 seconds. Then, at the 2006 World Athletics Final in Stuttgart, Germany, I finished sixth in the 100-meter hurdles. This race was my first taste at a world championship. Only the top eight hurdlers in the world get invited, so it was a big deal.

I also did well on the European circuit, with a win in Ostrava, Czech Republic. By the end of the 2006 season, I ranked fourth in the United States in the 100 meter and seventh in the world according to *Track & Field News*.

By 2006, I had started to make a real living. Back then the European track meets paid in cash. So after the meets, my agent would give me a thick envelope filled with euros. It got to the point where I was coming back to the United States with more cash than customs allowed.

One time I was so jet-lagged that on the last leg of the trip to Baton Rouge, I left my backpack on the plane. It had my prize money of $20,000 in euros, which was $10,000 more than was allowed.

Thankfully, the airline returned everything to me. Maybe they thought that stack of euro cash was Monopoly money because I never got in trouble for it. The point is, I started to make money. As I did, the intensity of training, traveling, and driving increased, while I was barely surviving the Louisiana heat.

In 2007, I won my first national championship at the USATF Indoor Championships in Albuquerque, New Mexico, smoking the 60-meter hurdles in 7.88 seconds. Then I won two meets at the European winter circuit and finished second in the 60-meter hurdles at two other meets.

Around this time, my contract with Nike was ending.

I remember waiting for a new offer. I was hopeful. But when it came, I again realized Nike wasn't nearly as invested in or as optimistic about my future as I was; the offer was insulting.

Coach Shaver reached out to the Nike representative to point out my increasing wins and to let them know that if they didn't do me better, it wouldn't be long before some other shoe company figured out what I was worth.

Nike didn't respond, didn't even check up on me.

Athletes having chips on their shoulders is a real thing. When I am giving everything I have physically, emotionally, mentally, and financially to be the best, and then feel disrespected by those who should know better, it drives me.

When I ran into the Nike rep at a meet in Monte Carlo and asked him about the contract, he said, "Why would we offer you more? We have the best athletes in the world, the best hurdlers. We don't need you."

That didn't sit well with me, to say the least. But I put my head down and just kept working.

I held on to the Nike contract for several months but didn't sign it. I just kept training and traveling and competing and sweating it out in my apartment as I worked my low-wage jobs and waited for the outdoor part of the season.

In April 2007 I crushed it. I won the 100-meter hurdles at the Drake Relays in my hometown of Des Moines. Then I finished third in the 100-meter hurdles at the USATF Outdoor Championships. That win earned me a spot on the US team at the IAAF World Championships in Osaka, Japan, where I took sixth place. I was running with the best in the world now, and I belonged. Even more, I knew I could win.

On the summer track circuit, I won meets at Rethymno, Greece, and Heusden-Zolder, Belgium, along with second-place finishes at Doha, Qatar; Sheffield, England; and Monaco.

I was winning.

And then I was offered a fat deal with ASICS, enough money for that financial breakthrough I'd been waiting for. With that, I was able to toss the Nike contract and quit all my jobs except one: hurdles.

I still have the scooter, by the way, although I did buy a car, a used Mercedes-Benz CLK 500. But not before I bought a town house. I wasn't going to be homeless ever again.

I didn't buy a new car, not because I couldn't afford it. I was making more than $100,000 a year at this point. I bought a used car because the economics major in me said, "Cars are your fastest depreciating items."

The ASICS sponsorship was the tipping point that ended my financial pressures and limitations so I could focus on hurdling like never before. And there was nothing I was more focused on than the 2008 Olympic trials.

I started the 2008 indoor season with second-place finishes in the 60-meter hurdles at events in Glasgow, Scotland; Gothenburg, Sweden; and Stuttgart, Germany. After picking up a win in Düsseldorf that set a meet record, I finished second in Karlsruhe with a personal best of 7.77 seconds. Susanna Kallur took first place with a world record time of 7.68 seconds.

My time was the second fastest an American had ever clocked. I was on fire.

I won my second straight national championship at the 2008 USATF Indoor Championships with a time of 7.88 seconds. And then, at the World Indoor Championships in Valencia, Spain, I won my first world championship in the 60-meter hurdles with a time of 7.80.

The Nike rep who said they sponsored the best hurdlers in the world? Yeah, not anymore.

Several months later, I was back at Hayward Field in Eugene, Oregon, for the 2008 Olympic trials, with Coach Shaver by my side.

And I won.

As Carol Lewis said then, I had been "around for years"! And I had been pushing for a breakthrough, athletically as well as financially. Missing out on the 2004 Games and then trying to find a decent sponsor led to hard days and a pretty big chip on my shoulder. But I leveraged them to push me toward Beijing in 2008, London in 2012, the Sochi Winter Games in 2014, and even further.

WORLD CHAMPION, AGAIN

In March 2010, Coach Shaver was in Fayetteville, Arkansas, for the NCAA Championships. I was in Doha, Qatar, competing in the 60-meter hurdles at the World Indoor Championships. I was focused on defending my world champion win from the year before. In the semifinal, though, I grazed a hurdle and barely qualified for the final. I was livid; I mean, I was the defending world champion.

Coach Shaver, who was still the head coach at LSU and my pro coach, couldn't travel with me in the early part of my pro track season because he had to finish out the collegiate season. In his place was my track agent, Paul Doyle, who served as the eyes and ears for Coach Shaver. Most agents are there to collect 10 to 20 percent of your earnings as they watch from the bleachers. But Paul did way more than most agents. He was in the warm-up areas, he walked me to the call rooms, and he did the job of coach, agent, and teammate. He's a great guy, and I have leaned on him over the years.

So when I was freaking out about grazing the hurdle and barely qualifying, unbeknownst to me, Paul called Coach Shaver. Because of the time difference, Paul had woken him up and told him, "Hey, Lolo was the last one to qualify, and she is a little worked up."

That was code for "Help!"

Then Paul handed me the phone.

I don't remember the specifics of what Coach said, but it wasn't one of those coaching aha moments, the ones you see in the movies where the athlete is like, "Yeah, that's exactly what I did wrong, and your insight will help me correct the error." He hadn't seen my race, so he couldn't exactly give me a coaching tip.

If you asked him now, he'd tell you, "I just made something up."

But I remember enough of what he said. It was some tough love and a reminder of who I was. Basically, he said, "You know how to run this race. Forget the race you just had, the hurdle you just grazed. Sh*t happens. So get your sh*t together and just go out and run this race."

It refocused me and gave me peace. It was what I needed.

I hung up the phone and broke records, running a 7.72 and winning the 60-meter world championship for a second time.

While I was on my victory lap, Paul called Coach Shaver and passed along the win and my time. Coach's response was "Bull!" I think he was more surprised than I was.

"Get your sh*t together" is a very important aspect of coaching. The good coaches know how to say this in a way their athletes can receive. Because sh*t happens. Sometimes you place ninth in the 2004 Olympic trials; sometimes you don't get that sponsorship; sometimes you don't get that job, that raise, that callback, that fill in the blank.

What is it you are pushing toward? Whatever it is, there will be times when your Nike equivalent won't respect you or recognize your worth, times when the system takes advantage of you, times when bad things happen. That's when you get to work.

I made $272,000 after winning that second indoor world championship race.

It was the most I'd ever won in a race. I'd broken the American record and the world championship record, and I became the first 60-meter female hurdler to defend her World Indoor title. The prize money was $40,000, but because I broke so many records, I also received bonuses that added up to a fat payday.

BREAKTHROUGH

I spent years in pursuit of a breakthrough. Yes, I was always pursuing my dream of the Olympics, but I was also breaking the cycle of poverty—both in my thinking and in my family line. The financial breakthrough was a huge deal for me. It was evidence of a truth I had been learning for years. It's called "sowing and reaping." God's faithfulness is very much connected to my work ethic.

Or as Coach Shaver calls it, "[taking] ownership of what it is that you're capable of doing."

Or as I call it, "hard work."

Breakthrough is a buzzword used to define a moment. But the word almost always represents and reveals a lifetime of intentional moments of hard work. There is no such thing as an instant breakthrough. It's the culmination of sweating and scootering and Home Depot. A breakthrough is simply the evidence of hard work.

While my breakthrough was making the Olympics and breaking world records, I want to highlight the financial breakthrough too, because it was no small thing to me. The Olympics was a defining moment in my life, but my financial breakthrough was what changed my life.

Breakthrough is a word we all love, especially in Christian circles. And God is the one we look to for breakthroughs. I believe that to the core of my being. But a pastor friend once told me, "Most of what we need in life God will give us. Most of what we want we have to go get."

God is my provider. He has proved it over the course of my life. Even when there wasn't enough, somehow there was enough. But that breakthrough has to be paid for; it has to be stewarded. I believe this is biblical. God is looking for people who will steward well the capabilities He gives us.

Jesus taught this principle when He told a parable about a wealthy man with three servants (Matthew 25:14–30). Before the man left on a trip, he entrusted each servant with a portion of his wealth. The man gave five bags of gold to the first servant, two bags of gold to the second servant, and one bag of gold to the third servant. The first two servants invested their gold in some way and doubled what was given to them. We don't know exactly what they did because Jesus didn't say, but we do know what the third servant did: he buried his gold.

When the wealthy man returned from his trip and asked for an accounting, he was displeased that the third servant hadn't used what he'd been given. What reason could the servant have had for not using what was entrusted to him?

"I was afraid," he said, "and went out and hid your gold in the ground. See, here is what belongs to you" (v. 25).

While God doesn't entrust us all with bags of gold, he does entrust us with talents, gifts, and natural abilities. And fear can keep us from using what God has entrusted to us, just as it did the unfaithful servant. We all have capabilities, and it's what we do with them that greatly determines whether or not we break through and achieve our goals.

God gives each of us abilities, but it's up to us to use them. I know, I have written on this already and will some more. It is the theme of my life and the key principle of this book. I keep emphasizing it because it's true.

In this chapter, I spent a good deal of time writing about the financial pressures I faced to highlight the broken Olympic system and the problematic foundational need for sponsorship. But while I think there needs to be more help for professional track and field athletes, I am all about playing the hand you're dealt and moving forward. And I've learned that my financial breakthrough is very much connected to taking ownership of what I am capable of doing.

I was an early adopter of the power of social media.

I spent a lot of time, and still do, responding to fans, updating photos, and telling people about my journey. Fans don't really know what Olympians do in between the Olympics; but it turns out, they want to know.

Between 2005 and 2010, people, athletes included, told me I was wasting my time with all the social media interaction. But flash-forward to 2021, when prize money for races has actually shrunk.[7] Social media is what has closed the financial gap and allowed me to maintain such a long career.

In 2005, I took ownership of my capabilities. I grew in ways you only can through hard work and perseverance. And in March 2010, I experienced a breakthrough financially.

I haven't looked back since.

SEVEN

AN INSPIRATION

After I turned pro, the first foreign country I traveled to was Germany. I don't count Canada because it's too close to the United States and it's a lot like Iowa. Also, the track teams I connect with most are usually Canadian. I like Canadians, I get along really well with Canadians, my massage therapist is Canadian, my writer friend is Canadian . . .

Now that I think about it, my first travel race in college was to Quebec, a truly beautiful city. Okay, Canada counts.

But my first all-pro race off the North American continent was in Germany. My agent at the time was German and got me in a lot of races there. Sometimes I'd be the only American competing.

I was excited about that first trip to Germany and kept telling everyone I was going to Suttenburg, which confused most people because there is no such city. I actually went to Stuttgart (pronounced "Schtut-gart"). I performed great, matching my fastest time, which was awesome. Another thing that was awesome: I had become a world traveler.

In the early days, most of my travels consisted of airports, hotels, track facilities, and maybe an after-race dietary splurge at McDonald's.

Don't judge me; I was young. On that first trip to Stuttgart, I didn't have Wiener schnitzel and schnapps. I had a *Hamburger Royal*, *pommes frites*, and *Kaffee*. That's German for a Quarter Pounder, fries, and coffee, which I knew because of the pictures on the menu.

At my first race, German athlete Tim Lobinger was over at the pole vault. He hit the bar at a huge height, and on the way down he yelled, *"Scheisse!"* I turned to my agent and asked, "What did he just scream?" My agent laughed and said, "Sh*t."

Ever since then, *scheisse* has been my cussword when I am trying not to cuss, which I often do and also try not to do. I know many Christians get a little bothered by strong language, so I try to be cautious. But I am an athlete who lives in a highly competitive world where emotions are extreme and expressive language is a way to release tension and also bond.

The only reason I even bring this up is because some people have questioned my faith and my convictions simply for cussing now and then. I think that's BS. One thing has nothing to do with the other. People get caught up in externals, but God "looks at the heart" (1 Samuel 16:7). That said, I do try to be sensitive when I think I should. So when I'm trying to express myself around sensitive people, I've found *scheisse* to be a great word.

Also, it's fun to say.

My early travels were well before Netflix and before I could afford a laptop. They were also the early days of cell phones. While I had one, there was no way I would turn it on unless I wanted to have a $1,000 bill when I got home.

So, to make a call, I would have to find an international call station or a computer lounge and use their computers for a series of fifteen-minute time allotments, which also cost money. You know what didn't cost money? Watching TV in my hotel room.

You don't truly know boredom until you've watched four hours of daytime German television.

In college I took Spanish as a minor and was pretty fluent. I'd discovered the best way to learn a language was to watch cartoons in the language you're studying. So I was always looking for Mickey, Donald, and Tom and Jerry.

While I was in Germany, I watched an episode in which Jerry was banging and pushing on a door, trying to get in, and on the other side Tom was banging and pushing on the door, trying to get out. But because they were both banging and pushing, no one was getting in or out. Classic. Hilarious.

Jerry was screaming, *"Lass mich rein!"* ("Let me in!")

Tom was screaming, *"Lass mich raus!"* ("Let me out!")

Oh, I just learned the words for "in" and "out," I thought. *I'm gonna use them.*

Later that day, an assigned German driver was taking me to the track meet in a passenger van. The driver passed by where the athletes needed to enter the stadium, where he was supposed to drop me off. And I thought, *Perfect opportunity to use the German I learned!*

But I got it a little mixed up.

I wanted to say, "Let me out." But instead, with growing insistence, I kept saying, "Let me in, let me in."

I continued to learn German, but as the days became months and the months became years, I found myself shuttled around by Dutch, Spanish, French, Arab, Finish, Swiss, and Chinese drivers. It was too many languages, and eventually the best I could do was learn the basics. You know, "Please," "Thank you," "I'm hungry," and "Where's the bathroom?"

Which made the night when I hit the ninth hurdle in Beijing even harder.

BEIJING

I cried for so long in the tunnel underneath the Beijing National Stadium that I missed the last bus that took the athletes back to the Olympic Village.

I had the little card every athlete had been given, which read, in Mandarin, "Take me to the Olympic Village." So I thought I was all set. I hailed a cab and read from my interpretation card.

But this cab driver must have been from some other city and on his first day of work. He had no idea what an Olympic Village was, let alone where to find it. And he didn't speak a word of English.

I sat in the back seat, emotionally and physically exhausted, knowing only one Mandarin word, *xiexie*, meaning both "hello" and "thank you," neither of which was helpful in getting me to my room.

While I felt very lost emotionally, the cab driver was literally lost. After an hour of him driving around and me pointing at the card and him having no clue what city he was in, I saw recognizable lights in the distance.

I pointed emphatically to them. "That's it, over there, stop, stop, let me out."

"*Lass mich raus!*"

"*Scheisse!*"

"*Xiexie.*"

When I finally walked into my room, I was emotionally and physically raw. And then I did what I had been doing for nearly eight years and what I do now, win or lose: I turned on my worship music and I praised God. I felt God's closeness and was reminded of what He said to me on the track only hours earlier: *But you're here.* And once again, I felt thankfulness and peace.

THE POST-RACE INTERVIEWS

In the same race in which I hit the ninth hurdle and lost in Beijing, my teammate Dawn Harper won gold. On the track, after that moment of great disappointment, after I'd been on my knees, and after God had settled my heart with those words *But you're here*, I got up and went to find Dawn to congratulate her.

I waited for her to take her victory lap, with no pain or bitterness in my heart.

As painful as it was to lose, especially the way I had, I felt a sense of peace and a sincere desire to congratulate her. She was my team-mate, which meant the United States had won a medal, and that was something we could all be proud of.

In 2008, I went to the Olympics thinking that what I'd watched on NBC for so many years was true—that we would all be team-mates, and we would all like one another and root for one another, even as we competed. I went into the Olympics thinking, *We're a team. We're Team USA.* I didn't get the medal, but we won as a team.

I was soon to learn a harsh lesson that would haunt me the rest of my career. In the Olympics, in track and field, in my experience, there's no such thing as teammates. Track and field is an individual sport, and it has often been a mean-girl situation, whether you par-ticipate or not. Also, in the end, only three medals are given out, and those three medalists, no matter what country they're from, will have more of a bond than you'll experience with your own team members.

While I waited for Dawn to take her victory lap so I could congratulate her, I was pulled away for a series of post-race interviews on the track and ended up missing the chance to connect with her in person.

During the interviews, I was raw and emotional, so my memory is somewhat of a blur. When NBC's Bob Neumeier asked if I could "put words" to what I was going through, I was composed. I said, "It's heartbreaking. I felt the gold around me, but it's hurdles, and if you can't finish the race, you're not supposed to be the champion."[1]

He asked about hitting the hurdle, and I talked about pulling away from the pack. I described how the hurdles were "coming up so fast" and how "normally I can turn it over and just keep up with the rhythm."[2]

He thanked me, and then I moved on to the next interview.

After an Olympic race there is a line of interviewers from every country, so it takes about ten minutes to work through them. Along the way, athletes are asked the same questions again and again.

By the time I got to the last interviewer, I was breathless and overwhelmed. When the fans cheered loudly at one of the events taking place behind me, the noise drowned out the interviewer's question, but I heard "What happened?"

I replayed it again: "The hurdles were just coming up very fast and I just told myself what I always tell myself, 'keep things tight.' But it's kind of like when you are racing a car and going max velocity and you hit a curve, either you can maintain control or you can crash and burn. Today I crashed and burned."[3]

I crashed and burned in the most important race of my life, I thought as the interviewer said something like, "It's so difficult—speed, finesse, jumping ability . . ."

Doing all I could not to fall apart, I responded, "You hit a hurdle about twice a year. It's just a shame it happened in the biggest race of my life . . . but what can you do but try again."[4]

The interviewer moved to his next question as the weight of disappointment crashed over me again. I heard him say, "The Olympic Games are all about the effort; sometimes the results just aren't there. Tell me about that effort, because I know you probably gave everything you had and then some. And that's what . . ."

The stadium was so loud, but his words echoed the devastating reality of the loss, and I began to fight back tears.

He continued, "That's what makes a moment like this so difficult." Then he paused. "Take a breath. Just talk to me when you're ready."

To this day, I can't watch this part of the interview, the pain was so raw.

With tears running down my face, I said, "You know, I wanted just to inspire people, really. And, um, you know, all I can tell people now, 'cause I can't inspire them to be a champion, I can just tell them, you know, life comes at you. You hit hurdles. Just pick yourself up again, 'cause right now it hurts, but tomorrow it's gonna hurt even more . . . and I'm just gonna pick myself up again. Hold my head up high. And just try again."

I openly mourned the loss, sincerely thanked God, congratulated my teammates, and looked with hope toward my future. It was heartbreaking, but I was sincere.

And although I had no idea at the time, the way I lost and how I conducted myself in the interviews elicited a great deal of empathy and interest among American viewers.

In those hours after the race, unbeknownst to me, my loss and then my interviews were becoming an inspiring Olympic story in the United States. While I was in the hotel, spending the next hours settling my heart, sportscasters across the country were replaying and commenting on my dramatic loss and the post-race interviews. Nearly twenty-eight million viewers in the United States had watched my heartbreaking loss and heard my raw emotion.

I am not taking credit for some great feat; it was God's grace. He filled me and spoke through me in those interviews. It was His peace I felt as I spoke. I am just trying to explain the odd phenomenon that occurred.

While I tried to recover in every way, I was unknowingly becoming a household name.

MCDONALD'S AND CANADIANS

After I'd spent some time in praise and worship, I was, in every way, exhausted—but I couldn't sleep. It was the middle of the night, and I was wide awake and restless. I had spent years working toward that moment on the track, and for better or worse, I had done my best. It was now behind me and, well, I was starving.

I went to the 24–7 McDonald's in the Olympic Village.

Obviously.

And, of course, it was full of Olympic athletes. What do all athletes do after their event is finished? They go to McDonald's. After months of living on a strict diet, McDonald's is like heaven.

What did I have? A Big Mac with fries and a Coke, plus five cheeseburgers, two apple pies, and a sundae.

Then I saw Dawn Harper.

This happened only hours after we'd raced. I was sitting down waiting for my order when I saw her get her food. I felt like the Holy Spirit was encouraging me to go talk to her, and since I had no ill feelings toward her—it's not like she was the reason I hit the hurdle—I went up to her table and congratulated her. She hardly acknowledged me and didn't make eye contact. It felt weird because she didn't invite me to sit, and she was incredibly reserved, which wasn't like Dawn because she has a bubbly personality. So I knew something was wrong. It felt like something toxic, but I couldn't imagine what it was and decided she was just tired.

I went back to my room, but I couldn't sleep. It was late when Angela Whyte texted me.

Angela is a Canadian hurdler, and we get along really well. I had literally just competed against her in the 100 meter. She hadn't medaled either and also couldn't sleep. So we joined up and did what Olympic athletes do: find something else we could direct our competitive drive toward.

Every Olympic Village has a game room where athletes can go before and after a race and hang out. There's a rec room with arcades and carnival games and basketball; we played basketball.

I don't remember who won, which reveals either how aimless and unfocused I was or that I lost and forgot. I do remember us making jokes about how we were both losers, though.

I didn't go out to the Olympic parties, but I also never slept that night. And as the sun was breaking, my agent called and told me I had been requested for an interview. I had no idea what it was about; I just followed his instructions.

So, instead of crashing, I found myself, red-eyed, on the Olympic set of Today with Matt Lauer. I was sitting in a chair next to Dawn Harper, and we were being interviewed together.[5]

Why?

That's a good question. One I have asked many times since. And Dawn has as well.

I had lost; she had won. I had no idea why I was there. I assumed it was because Dawn and I were teammates.

I sat waiting for the interview to begin, uncomfortable because I had lost and because I knew something was up between Dawn and me. She seemed angry.

The interview started with Matt Lauer congratulating Dawn and then saying the oddest thing: "This is one of those stories that's tough to tell, but let's start with your side of it."

While that statement is true if you're interviewing me, it's ridiculous if you're interviewing Dawn. Then Lauer went on to tell Dawn she ran a great race and asked her how it felt to stand on the podium.

Dawn answered as I once again wondered why I was there.

Matt's second question was about whether Dawn knew what was happening in the competition. "Do you have to focus so much on your own hurdle that you don't even really know what happens with Lolo?"

Matt was asking Dawn questions about me. As I was sitting there, hearing her respond, I began to get a small sense of what was brewing. In hindsight, I now know I was there because of the way I had lost—it was heartbreaking not only for me but for many viewers—and because of the gracious and genuine way I had handled Dawn's win in my post-race interviews. Unbeknownst to me, those interviews had been making for better television than Dawn's win.

That wasn't fair to Dawn or, honestly, to me. But it's what happened.

Trust me, neither Dawn nor I wanted this narrative. I wanted to win, and to this day would trade all the positive press for a medal. And Dawn wanted the respect of having medaled without having to talk about Lolo Jones.

While I'd had no idea of the impact my loss—or my response to it—had on viewers around the world at the time, I was picking up on the impact it was having on Dawn.

Lauer went on to ask Dawn a profoundly thoughtless question: "In entering the race knowing [Lolo] was the favorite, did you have silver in your mind or something else?"

As an Olympic hurdler I can say with absolute certainty that the question is unfathomable and highly insulting. There is no such thing as an Olympic athlete who goes into any race thinking about placing second.

Scheisse, what a stupid question.

When my questions came, I answered them as honestly and respectfully as I could. I spoke about how heartbreaking it was to lose but also how thankful I was to have been there and how I hoped to get another shot at winning a medal in four years' time.

Matt loved my responses and praised me for my attitude. "That's the best attitude I've heard in a long time, Lolo. That's fantastic."

They *were* good responses and a good attitude; God's grace was speaking through me. But the problem was, Matt seemed more excited about my answers than Dawn's gold medal.

By the time the interview ended, I could tell Dawn was angry at the fact that I was there, which she has since confirmed. And it makes sense. In hindsight, I wish I had said no to the interview as it infringed on Dawn's spotlight. But I was young and obediently went where I was told. I also had no idea of the growing narrative in the United States. So for me, I wasn't fake or looking to be in the spotlight as I have since been accused of. I was doing the same thing Dawn was doing: responding to questions.

However, there was one main difference. I was answering questions after a crushing loss; Dawn was answering questions after a hard-run, well-earned win. Both of us had gone into those games with an Olympic dream. Dawn's came true, and she earned it. Mine didn't. So while I understood Dawn's anger after that interview, I couldn't understand why it was directed at me.

Unfortunately, that interview and the way the race was reported afterward affected our professional relationship and hugely impacted the days leading up to the 2012 Games four years later.

Over the twenty-four hours after that race, it was difficult to navigate her escalating anger directed at me. The humbler I was in interviews, the more it seemed to infuriate her.

I was interviewed several times, and I was honest and vulnerable about my experience, but I also made sure to praise Dawn and the other winners. "I know the two other girls who medaled, and you know what, they are great girls and they deserve that medal."[6]

I was asked time and again if I would have won had I not hit the ninth hurdle, and my answer was always some version of "You know, it's the hurdles. It's not the 100 [meter]. They put the hurdles there for a reason. You have to get over them. If you can't get over them, you're not meant to be the champion."

That's obviously true, and so, as hard as it was to lose because I hit a hurdle, it wasn't hard to say. But that's not the story the press wanted to tell.

In one interview, the interviewer actually suggested that my loss, and how I handled it, was more inspiring to Americans than if I had won. I thought he was confused about how things worked for an athlete in the Olympics; I wasn't there to lose.

But I was getting my first glimpse into another outcome. He was right. My loss had inspired.

Then the interviewer asked, "Do you understand at this point, can you understand, the amazing impact you've had on us, on America, on everyone that's watching? Maybe even more so than if you were standing on a medal stand. . . . You were expected to win that medal. What happened there was not expected, and you've made a tremendous impact on our country. Can you fathom that?"[7]

I actually teared up as I tried to respond. The idea that I was an inspiration encouraged me. I couldn't fully fathom how it was possible, not yet, but it was something I had literally prayed the night before.

THE PRAYER

I have never prayed to win a race. It doesn't make sense. I mean, there are seven other girls, and they are all praying too. I see them in the call room, on the track. They're all praying. I mean, how does God choose?

So I've never done those last-minute Hail Mary prayers on the track. Before a race I have one obsession: win. So if I prayed then, it would feel like I saw God as some good luck charm. I've never wanted God to be my good luck charm.

However, the night before a race, in my hotel room, I would often watch a scene from the 2006 high school football movie *Facing the Giants*. In that movie the coach says to his team, "If we win, we praise Him, and if we lose, we praise Him."[8] And that is my prayer.

My prayers have always been, *God, whether I win or lose, use my talents to the best of my abilities because You created me for this*. I feel like that's a good prayer because it's honest. I want to use everything He created me for to the very best of my ability.

But before the 2008 Olympic finals, I had an addition to my prayer. I felt grateful for the opportunity to represent the USA, and I remember vividly praying, *God, this is the biggest platform I'll ever have in my life. Let me use this platform to inspire people, whatever the outcome*.

My prayer was that I would be an inspiration. That's what I wanted to be. *God, use me to be an inspiration for people on how to overcome.* But let's be real, it was a cheat prayer. I was praying to win.

In my mind, being an inspiration meant winning an Olympic medal. I mean, what's more inspiring than coming out of poverty, making the team, and then winning? Everyone loves a good underdog story.

However, in a million years, I never imagined that losing would be how I would inspire people.

God answered my prayer. I lost in such a noteworthy fashion that I inspire people to this very day. People still let me know how inspiring I was when I lost the Olympics.

In my life I have given more interviews than I can count, but there are two that I believe have been God-breathed. The first was the last post-race interview I gave, the interview on the track directly after the event where I had tears in my eyes and the pain was at its most visceral yet I believed God was still good. I was heartbroken but also thankful and hopeful.

The second was five years later. I was at the Ravens–49ers Super Bowl game in New Orleans, doing press for the 2014 Olympic bobsled team, when Skip Bayless of ESPN's *First Take* asked a question I wasn't expecting.

Skip Bayless: Lolo, I've always respected the fact that you've been very public about the role that God plays in your life. Now we have Ray Lewis as the focal point of this Super Bowl. And he continues to talk about how it has been "God's will," to quote Ray, that the Ravens have won three playoff games and will win the Super Bowl. How do you feel about "God's will" deciding games?

My answer was as God-inspired an answer as I've ever given. And it was built on the heartbreaking loss I'd experienced in 2008 and the four years of hard work and struggle that followed.

> **Me:** Uh, . . . that's a very tough one for me. I feel like there's been times where I felt like it was God's will for me to have a successful season, but I have also felt like it was God's will as well to help me to learn from certain losses. . . . I don't think God cares about a certain game, or race, or performance, but He does care about the condition of our heart. And so, I hope that, like, whether we have success or we have failures that we always rely on Him for our strength . . . during the whole process.[9]

I don't believe God plays a role in who wins and loses. God didn't make me hit that hurdle. But I do believe God answers prayers. By that I mean, "In all things God works for the good of those who love him." That's the promise of Romans 8:28.

I don't know how it works, but I know God can redeem and restore and work the hard things, the failures and the broken places, for good.

Good isn't always evidenced in wins. Sometimes "good" is what you learn in losing. Good is sometimes about losing in a way that releases grace and hope and trust; it's about what inspires the world around us. I think good is ultimately about what I told Skip Bayless: the condition of our hearts. And the condition of our hearts is often discovered and revealed in the most heartbreaking ways.

I have a friend who says, "I got squeezed and Jesus came out."

Life does that; it squeezes us.

Even though I wanted to win, even though my heart was convinced that inspiration would come through winning, when I got squeezed, Jesus came out. And Jesus really is amazing. He wins at everything, even losing.

Seriously, Jesus literally died on a cross, and in so doing, He won. Sometimes God isn't playing the game we are playing. But His love and goodness always win.

The cool thing about laying down your life for God, which He tells us to do in Matthew 16:24, is that even when you lose, you win. If there's a takeaway from this chapter, it's simply this: when you give God your life and your dreams, even when you lose, you win.

I truly did not want to inspire people by losing, but I can see how I did. Because my heart was set on representing God well, even when I lost, He won, and ultimately, in an odd and hard way, so did I. It's just a matter of distance and perspective.

After the devastating loss of 2008, my career rose to new levels, and I experienced opportunities I never would have had otherwise. Sometimes how God answers our prayers is radically different from what we would have thought. But He is faithful and He is good.

If you had told me the night before the 2008 Games that I'd someday be writing a book that hopefully encourages and inspires people, I would have told you my grades in high school English didn't support it. Then I would have imagined that it meant I had won an Olympic medal, maybe even two.

But here we are. As of right now, I have no Olympic medals. Still, here I am, writing a book that I hope inspires you.

If it hasn't yet, no worries, 'cause this *scheisse* is about to get real.

EIGHT

WAITING, DATING, AND TRUSTING

In 2012 and 2013, I did a series of interviews on the London Olympics with Mary Carillo for HBO's *Real Sports with Bryant Gumbel*. Those interviews are kinda famous because, well, we spent a lot of time on a subject other than the Olympics: my dating life.

Or more to the point, my sex life.

Or more to the point, my lack thereof.

Mary Carillo: Lolo, you've told the Twittersphere that you're a virgin.

Me: Yeah, my hands were shaking when I did that.[1]

Earlier in 2012, a follower on Twitter asked me a question. It was one I got all the time: "Why don't you ever have a boyfriend?" or "Why aren't you dating?"

And for better, and also for worse, I answered it.

I told my Twitter follower and the world that I was waiting, that I wanted to save my virginity for my husband. I was nervous. I knew my answer was countercultural. I expected it could open up a conversation, but I wasn't looking to make the news. I promise you, I wasn't trying to be the poster child for some abstinence movement, and I never thought I'd later spend so much time on HBO discussing it.

It went viral, as they say. It was a story, and it was everywhere. Which is why Mary was asking me about it.

My decision to practice abstinence was front-page news.

Seriously, if I'd tweeted that I'd cured cancer or solved Amelia Earhart's disappearance or discovered time travel, I would have received less attention.

Some people were even referring to it as an announcement, as though I'd called a press conference.

Can you imagine?

"Hello, thank you for coming on such short notice. I want to announce that I may have shocking views on sex that may differ from others."

Billy, with *Sensationalism News*, says, rather bored, "I doubt it. We've heard every view on sex that exists and nothing shocks us anymore, but we're here. So how do you view sex differently?"

"Thank you for asking, Billy." I always do my best to learn every reporter's name.

I take a deep breath. I've thought long and hard about this announcement. "I have decided to wait until I am married."

Suddenly the room explodes into a mass of reporters asking why, with tones ranging from confused amusement to condescending offense to disgusted outrage.

Yeah, I understand how Twitter works, but I really didn't think anyone was going to care.

Now back to my real-life interview with Mary Carillo.

Me: I've always been open and honest about who I am, and
  I share openly on social media. Sometimes I'm accused
  of actually oversharing.
Mary Carillo (laughing): Well, a lot of people don't discuss
  their virginity publicly.
Me: Yeah, I know.
Mary Carillo: Don't you think at times maybe you *could be*
  oversharing?[2]

That was a fair question. And one that has been asked more often in
the years since.

Do I regret being so forthcoming on Twitter about waiting to
have sex until after I am married?

No.

And yes.

There have been pluses to sharing. I was flooded with support
from others who were practicing abstinence, and it encouraged me
to know I wasn't alone. Because I certainly felt alone.

And it was good to know I had encouraged those who also felt
alone; those who, like me, live in a culture that increasingly demands
acceptance of sex outside of marriage while at the same time having
no value or respect for anyone who choose otherwise.

And finally, it made my dates easier. Kinda.

In the past, I'd often feel the pressure to figure out when and how
to awkwardly tell the guy that we were not going to have sex. But
suddenly, thanks to Twitter and news outlets around the world, my
dates knew beforehand that sex was off the table.

So, yeah, there were upsides to sharing my values. But let's just say, if I *had* discovered time travel, after I went back and cleanly cleared that ninth hurdle, I'd likely not share so openly with that guy on Twitter about my dating life.

Why?

First, my dates seemed to ultimately become more focused on my beliefs about sex than, you know, dating. Theoretically, the guy who already knows my values and still asks me out would hold the same values, right? Wrong. I soon discovered that most guys didn't believe me. They thought I was lying. Or worse, they approached my virginity as a challenge.

Here's how I explained it to Mary Carillo: "When you tell a guy you're a virgin, and this is the honest truth, . . . they say, 'Okay, I respect that.' But you can already see it in their mind and in their eyes that they're like, 'She's lying about this, and I'll crack it.' So after we talk a month or so, you know, usually a month to three months, they're like, 'Oh, shoot, she was serious. Time for me to exit.'"[3]

Second, I am mocked endlessly. I've literally had people say I lost the Olympics because I was a virgin. That's just dumb. For every encouragement I've received, there are a hundred trolls who ridicule me with the most horrific attacks: "No guy wants you." "If you had sex, you'd be nicer." "Girl, dust the cobwebs off." "You're too old."

That last one stings the most, because it touches on the disheartening reason why I wouldn't be as forthcoming today if I had a do-over. You see, I gave those interviews when I was twenty-nine and thirty. When I shared my decision, I figured I'd be married soon. But almost a decade later, I am still single and still a virgin. And that was never the plan.

I had hoped I would be married with kids by now. But life doesn't always go as I plan or hope for, and I find my faith being stretched as I write this chapter. And, even though it has been really hard and I am really disappointed, I choose to still wait.

I told Mary, "I want to wait till I'm married to have sex. My mom, she was with my dad for twenty years and they never got married, and they're not together anymore. So I just want . . . to have that solid bond. It's just . . . a gift I want to give to my [future] husband.

"Please understand, this journey [to wait until I am married] has been hard. . . . It's the hardest thing I've ever done in my life, harder than training for the Olympics, harder than graduating from college. . . . I've been tempted. I've had plenty of opportunities."[4]

But I live in a world that doesn't get it. The idea that someone would save themselves for marriage isn't even considered old-fashioned anymore; it's considered absurd and dumb.

SETTING THE RECORD STRAIGHT: IT'S ABOUT TRUST

I was on the TV show *Celebrity Big Brother* several years ago. It was an experience.

While on the show, I was talking with Kandi Burruss, a Christian and a show member, who didn't understand why I was waiting. She asked a question I get all the time: "What about sexual compatibility? You could end up married to a guy with a small package."

It was such a strange and revealing question, as though sex is nothing more than a pleasurable experience. You know, like eating ice cream. And marriage is nothing more than an absurd contract that locks you into one flavor, like spending the rest of your life stuck with pistachio.

In our culture today, we ignore the emotional, relational, and spiritual dynamics of a sexual relationship, and instead we dumb it down to nothing more than a pleasurable transaction between two people.

"I am a virgin, so how would I know the difference?" I replied. She didn't seem to get it, so I continued, "Do you remember your first kiss and how excited you were? Your heart was beating and it was amazing, right? Looking back, were you a good kisser?"

She laughed and shook her head no.

"Me neither. I literally thought I had to take the rubber bands out of my braces so we could kiss. I had no clue what I was doing. I was terrible. But it was my first kiss, so, to me, it was pretty amazing. It wasn't until I had more kisses and more experiences that I realized how bad that first kiss was. . . . So, yeah, I'm not worried about bad sex or small packages, because I have never had sex."

My point? Even though I wasn't good at it, my first kiss was an amazing experience because I had nothing to compare it with. My lack of experience protected me.

To me, when it comes to sex, the spirit of comparison leads to superficial concerns about sexual compatibility and package size. And these concerns are so far removed from the innocence and intimacy sex was always meant to protect and express, so far from what really matters to me.

What really matters to me? Why am I waiting?

Let me set the record straight. Ready?

I have never investigated becoming a nun. I want to have sex. But I am waiting because my greatest desire is more than just to have sex.

I want to experience trust. And everything that comes with it.

Stick with me.

The fact is, you can have sex without trust. But you can't have intimacy without trust. You can't build a deep, long-lasting, healthy friendship with your husband or wife without trust. You can't experience and create a healthy family without trust.

That's what I want. It's what I have always wanted.

Trust is earned. It's developed through faithfulness and commitment over time. Trust is only as deep as the commitment. And marriage is one of the most beautiful expressions of faithfulness and commitment: "To have and to hold, *till death us do part*." It's literally a commitment that is intended to span the entirety of life. And only within the context of that life commitment is trust given the best chance to deepen and thrive.

You know, waiting to have sex until marriage is God's idea. While His ideas may be old-fashioned, they are never naive, foolish, or ignorant. God's ideas on marriage are meant to provide a safe context so that trust, intimacy, and family can be experienced to its fullest. Love, marriage, and then sex. That's God's order. And I believe I have the best chance at creating a healthy family when I follow that order.

Which is why I am still waiting.

Sex is an intimate act shared between two people. I think that when it's shared outside of trust, outside of marriage and a lifelong commitment, it's simply an imitation of intimacy, and it can actually lead to a broken and fractured ability to trust. I've seen this play out in the lives of family and friends.

I know many will say, "You can be married and still have broken trust."

Of course. Life has hurdles, and marriage does as well. But I believe you have a better chance of building or rebuilding trust when you're married than when you're just hooking up.

Others will say, "You don't have to be married to develop trust."

That may be true. But I grew up in a house where Mom and

Dad didn't get married, where trust was fractured, and they are no longer together. A number of studies have found that living with someone before marriage actually increases the chance of divorce or separation.[5]

That's the opposite of what I want. I know the emotional insecurity of growing up in a house with fractured trust, and I don't want that for myself or my future kids.

> **Mary Carillo:** When I put together your whole life and what you've been through, and you've had traumas and you've had this unstable existence for such a long time, it actually makes sense to me that you want to have the kind of family that you wish you'd had as a kid.
>
> **Me:** Yeah, . . . I guess I want that Norman Rockwell picture.[6]

I do. I want the Norman Rockwell picture—a husband who loves well, a man I can partner with to have a family where love and trust are daily expressions of life. And I want sex; I want ice cream and all the flavors with one man. I believe you can actually experience the best sex in the context of marriage.

A friend of mine, who has been married for twenty-five years and counting, recently told me that the night before he got married, the night before he first had sex, his dad said to him, "If you do this right, if trust and faith [are] your foundation, you will have the best sex of your life in your forties, fifties, and sixties."

Then my friend smiled and said, "My dad was right."

I've talked to enough married friends who can attest to the fact that sex is more meaningful, beautiful, exciting, and intimate as the years pass. You can discover true compatibility over a lifetime of faithfulness, where trust is protected and developed.

And that's what I want.

Christian writer and pastor Charles Stanley once said something like, "Our willingness to wait reveals the value we place on the object we're waiting for."

I value my virginity because I value what it represents. I'm willing to wait for sex because my future husband, even though I don't know him yet, is the most valuable person I will have a relationship with besides my family. He and I will have kids. He will be the person I live with twenty-four hours a day, 365 days a year. That is worth the wait.

So let me set the record straight. Not having sex has been hard. I have come close a few times, and I have questioned if waiting is worth it. I'm human and I have desires. But I am waiting for the kind of sex that is experienced within the faithful, lifelong commitment of marriage. I want intimacy. I want friendship, connection, and the kind of sex that happens only inside the commitment of two becoming one and sharing a life together. I want sex inside of trust.

WHAT ABOUT GOD?

I know some of you are wondering how my faith has influenced my decision to wait, so let me address that.

At the very beginning of the Bible, God laid out his thoughts about marriage: "A man leaves his father and mother and is united to his wife, and they become one flesh. Adam and his wife were both naked, and they felt no shame" (Genesis 2:24–25). I think maybe the Creator of the universe understands how relationships and family and trust work best, and He designed a way for us to experience those things fully.

But the fact is, I made the decision to wait until marriage when I was a kid, during the unstable years of my childhood, long before I understood what the Bible said about it. The Bible is pretty clear on waiting, and it has helped me at times to know that I am within the will of God for my life. But at this point, words on the page of a book, even the Good Book, aren't what sustain me.

The Bible is always meant to introduce us to the Author. And the more I get to know the Author, the more time I spend with Him, the more convinced I am that everything He does is about faith, about trust.

Which is why, if I am being honest, when it comes to marriage, I am kinda mad at God these days. I am mad at God because I want a husband who loves God and me completely and wholly, and I feel like He put that desire in my heart when I was a little girl. But it hasn't happened yet.

I have kept a journal most of my life, and as I prepared to write this chapter, I went back to it. I read through my college years all the way back to middle school, and I found dreams and prayers for a husband and a family. And I feel like, "God, you put this desire in my heart way back then. Why am I still single when I have wanted a family more than anything else?"

Years ago, I was encouraged when a preacher quoted Jeremiah 29:11: "'For I know the plans I have for you,' declares the LORD, 'plans to prosper you and not to harm you, plans to give you hope and a future.'" When I hear that verse now, I get discouraged, and then I get mad at God. And I know that's stupid, because He's God. But let's not pretend I am more than human. I don't understand His plan. And that's the problem.

A FRAGILE FAITH

Have you ever been mad at God? If you said yes, thanks for being honest.

I think it comes from the deep disappointment we feel when every part of us desires an answer but it doesn't come. The kind of disappointment that is years in the making. The kind of disappointment we joke about because what else can we do?

I've been making jokes for years. Here's one I shared with Mary Carillo back in 2012: "I'm one year out from turning thirty, so I say if they're making a sequel to *The 40-Year-Old Virgin*, . . . I am their candidate. . . . I'm a little bit awkward like Steve Carell. I could definitely play that role."[7]

I am closer to forty now, so that joke is way less funny because it's becoming my reality. I made that joke almost ten years ago.

I get mad at God, and I'm guessing you do too.

But this is about me.

I was asked recently why I wouldn't just walk away from God if I'm so mad at Him. If you have never met God, I understand the question. But I have met Him.

I could never walk away from God. I have known His presence, and there is nothing truer, nothing more beautiful and good. There is nothing more sustaining than God's peace and joy. I have literally been pressed to the floor, humbled on my face, while experiencing God's love for me. I've known His love and grace and kindness. He has been my Savior, Lord, Father, and Friend.

God is the creator of the universe, and while I may not be able to theologically break this all down for you, I know without a shadow of a doubt that God is powerful, that He is not against me, and that His plans for me are good.

That's what makes my deepest disappointment even more hurtful, and why I get mad at Him.

My earthly father? He doesn't have that much power. You know, he was locked up a lot, so I couldn't hold it against him if he didn't show up to my track meets. But when you see how powerful God is and you experience Him in your life, when He has provided for you miraculously in so many ways, it hurts when it seems like He is ignoring you.

Add to that, I often feel like an idiot around the subject of waiting, like a worldwide laughingstock. People have harshly mocked me because of the stance I've taken. I have been ridiculed for being a virgin, and it's like, "Where are you, God?"

Is this too real?

The fact is, there are a lot of books out there for twentysomething Christian singles, but not many for thirtysomething ones. Maybe because we are all a little exhausted and mad, and our stories aren't tidy enough to sell. Maybe because, as I told Mary Carillo, "When I was twenty-two, twenty-four, it was cute. Like, 'Oh I'm a virgin,' you know, that's cute. At twenty-four to twenty-nine, it's not cute. Like, you get judged a lot."[8]

In my late thirties? I don't know. Lately my faith is a little fragile around the subject of waiting. And so what is left for me to do?

Trust.

Maybe faith is about living sure in God's goodness even when the answer evades us. Maybe faith is about not knowing but still trusting in the goodness of God. Maybe faith is at its most powerful when it's fragile.

Just writing that makes me mad.

In so many things, I have discovered that if I do the work, if I don't quit, I can achieve success. I can get the answer.

But I have done the work, I haven't quit, and I still don't have the answer in the husband department. All I have is my experience with a loving God and my fragile faith that He is good even when I don't understand, even when I don't have the answers.

And I do believe this. I have seen and experienced this truth in so many ways throughout my life. I know God loves me and only has goodness and love for me. So when I find myself unable to comprehend my disappointments, I still have my fragile faith.

Let me express some of this fragile faith for you. I hope it encourages you in the area of your greatest disappointment. I hope it encourages your trust.

This is what I think: God can handle my anger. And yours.

This is what I am convinced of, even though it's painful to write: I don't know what my future holds, but God is still good.

I believe there is life in that belief. And maybe that's faith.

Maybe faith isn't about what I can understand. Maybe it's about trusting that God is good even when I can't understand.

And then going out on another date.

MR. RIGHT

Now that we understand I would rather not be the poster child for abstinence until marriage, now that we're clear I do want to have sex but only in the context of a trusting, loving marriage, and now that we are on the same page about the fragility of faith and the goodness of God, let's talk about the perfect guy.

You know, "The one."

Okay, so I don't actually believe in "the one." At least, not until I'm married. Then I absolutely believe in "the one." And I think he's out there. In fact, if he is reading this right now, "Hey, call me."

A lot of guys are players, but I know a guy is interested if he pursues me. I will put myself in a position to be pursued. I really like it when the guy makes the effort.

That hasn't changed since high school.

I was a tomboy who grew up with three brothers. I had really curly hair. I didn't know how to dress and didn't have girly instincts. I would wear my brothers' clothes to school sometimes because we didn't really have a lot of clothes. And it was the '90s, so baggy was in. As for hair and makeup, forget about it. I never wore my hair down; every day it was in a bun or a ponytail. That's all I knew.

Freshman year in high school, girls were starting to get boy crazy. But that really didn't register for me. Looking back, I realize there were some boys who flirted with me, but I wasn't paying attention, I guess. *Clueless* might be the right word. I was an athlete, and most of my focus was there.

Also, until my senior year when I got braces, I had a huge gap between my front teeth. So while I wasn't ugly, I didn't look the way I do now. Today I've graced the covers of magazines, so I've learned about makeup and hair. And I am a lot more girly.

I didn't have a date until my senior year, and it wasn't because someone asked me out. I actually asked the guy I liked to the prom.

I have since been on some really good dates and some really bad ones. I have also dated some really good men and some two-faced hypocrites. I know, this is where you are hoping I'll dish. You probably want to know about that famous football player or basketball player or baseball player.

But I'm gonna practice healthy hindsight. You remember when I talked about how we should focus on God's love for us, His faithfulness, His protection, and so on?

I have been hurt a couple of times, and once by a famous guy who actually told me I wasn't famous enough for him to date. But it won't help you or me to tell you who that man was; he knows.

So what does a good date look like for me?

First, the date doesn't have to be with a famous guy. I am looking for someone who has a relationship with God and shares my values. I am not looking for someone who is *open* to my faith. I am looking for someone who knows Jesus, who walks with God.

I've been asked if it matters if he is a virgin. No. But it matters that he is practicing abstinence now. I want a man of integrity, not someone who gives lip service to being a Christian but isn't living like one, who isn't actually kind or generous, or who has an ego the size of Texas.

Anyway, I want a man who has self-control. A man of character who values himself and the woman he is with. A man who is focused on a future and not just the moment. I am not looking for the perfect man, because he doesn't exist. But it would be nice if the guy I'm with is working on being a good man.

Second, I like dates where we can do something together. Coffee is a great first date; it's casual and gives us both an opportunity to bail if it's not working. And games, I like games. But maybe we shouldn't play games on the first date, because I'm just the teeniest bit competitive.

Finally, and I think this is what we all want, I like dates that are comfortable. I'm looking for someone I can wear sweatpants with while lying on the couch and watching old episodes of *Downton Abbey* or *90 Day Fiancé*.

It's about friendship. It's about doing the boring daily things with and knowing you would rather be there than anywhere else.

It's about trust, right?

That's why I am waiting.

UNAPOLOGETICALLY COUNTERCULTURAL

At this point, you guys know I am not big on regret; instead, I try to use my past to make a future.

So, ultimately, I don't regret tweeting about my decision to wait. On that day I discovered I was not alone, while at the same time I became a voice for so many who are living counter to culture, and so many more who want to wait but have felt culturally pressured to be sexually active.

In a day when it's actually more acceptable to release a sex tape than to tell people you're waiting, I am unapologetically fighting for a marriage where trust, intimacy, and family can be experienced to the fullest.

In a day when marriages fail and families are struggling like never before, I hope my words and actions inspire you to fight for your marriage and family now and in the future.

Waiting has been hard, a countercultural fight for sure. And because I live in a world that mocks my conviction, I've taken some punches. But I'm not throwing in the towel.

I've lived intentionally, sharing my story along the way, with my faith always front and center.

While I understand people might attack me for my beliefs, and while I have faced my deepest disappointments in this area of my life, I haven't changed my mind.

I am unapologetically countercultural. I am still standing, still learning how to trust, and still believing that God is faithful.

NINE

WITHOUT VISION

People probably don't realize exactly how badly you were hurting."

ESPN made that statement in a 2011 interview shortly after I had spinal surgery. Yeah, spinal surgery.

"I was miserable," I said. "It was awful. At first, it was just when I was running, but then it was when I was walking. And sitting. And sleeping. I couldn't sit longer than forty minutes without being in pain. I remember being on a date—a hot date!—this past summer. We went to watch the *Transformers* movie, which has to be the longest film ever. And I kept squirming in my seat because it hurt too much to sit still. I had to keep getting up and stretching my back every thirty minutes. It kind of ruined the date, I have to say."[1]

In 2011, I had competed in three meets, hitting a hurdle in each one.

"I can count on one hand the number of hurdles I hit in a year, including practices. So there was clearly something going on that I had to address," I said.[2]

I failed to advance out of the semifinals in the 100-meter hurdles at the 2011 USATF Outdoor Championships, which meant I didn't qualify for the World Athletics Championships (formally IAAF World Outdoor Track and Field Championships), a heat I'd run in for the last several years.

I wanted to compete in the 2012 Olympics, but I was in so much pain, I could barely get out of bed.

Every nerve in my body was on fire. It felt like I was living out a torture scene in a prisoner-of-war movie. The pain was so intense that I gladly would have given up the colonel's secret recipe or the location of Wakanda—heck, I would have confessed to being the second shooter on the grassy knoll just to make it stop. It was painful not only physically but also emotionally.

There was clearly something wrong with me, but the doctors couldn't tell me what it was. I was experiencing a sharp shooting pain down my legs and numbness in my feet, and it was scary, both in my everyday life and in my career. It's really hard to hurdle at an Olympic level when you can't feel your toes.

I had met with several doctors and had several MRIs, with no answers. At the time, I was sponsored by Red Bull. They had me see their neurological spinal specialist in California, Dr. Robert Bray.

At first he thought it might be some rare virus from Africa, because, well, when you don't know what's wrong, it could be anything, including, apparently, a rare virus from Africa. It wasn't.

This all led to me lying on a table in a sterile medical facility with pins piercing my body.

They were lighting up my nerves to "extract information." That's not a medical term. It's the kind of thing a secret agent says, but I didn't have any information to give them and would make a horrible secret agent. It hurt so bad I thought I was going to die.

And I was afraid. I was beat up, exhausted, and running out of diagnoses.

What if this doesn't work? What if we still don't have any answers? What if . . .

PEACE BEYOND UNDERSTANDING

The apostle Paul wrote, "Do not conform to the pattern of this world, but be transformed by the renewing of your mind. Then you will be able to test and approve what God's will is" (Romans 12:2). I wanted to know God's will. So I decided to fast and pray.

Jesus prayed and fasted, so I believe in prayer and fasting.

Fasting is a discipline that helps me gain clarity. It helps me put aside every distraction so I can discern God's thoughts. I don't believe God requires us to fast for Him to speak to us, but when you're afraid and desperate and don't feel like you can hear Him, you do whatever you can think of to get answers.

I wanted to hear God's voice. I wanted to know if my track career was over. I wanted the pain to end. I wanted God to give wisdom to the doctors so they could find what was wrong with me. I wanted God's healing.

Fear is often connected to an unpredictable future, and mine was very much in question. I wanted answers.

Will I be able to compete for a spot on the 2012 Olympic team?

Is my career over?

Will I get married? Do I have a future husband?

Those questions haunted my every moment, and as you already know, the husband question still haunts me. The desires of our hearts are always juxtaposed against the painful possibility that we will not see them fulfilled. That's life. It's also where we discover faith.

But this juxtaposition was messing with me and my faith.

My fast started with three days of no food and water, and then, after that, chicken broth. I was on my second week of the fast when I found myself lying on a table in a sterile medical facility willingly submitting myself to torture with needles.

That night I went back to my hotel room exhausted and in a fragile mental state. As soon as I walked in the door, I fell to my knees and cried out to God. Instantly I felt Him fully present.

It's hard to explain, but the best words I can think of are *love* and *peace*. I knew I was deeply loved by God, and I felt peace. There's a verse in Philippians that captures what I felt: "The peace of God, which transcends all understanding, will guard your hearts and your minds in Christ Jesus" (4:7). I once heard a pastor say, "This peace is only available to someone who is in a circumstance beyond their ability to understand." I experienced that peace.

Then I sensed God speak to me: *Two thousand and twelve is going to be fine.* Again, it's hard to explain, but hearing God speak is more like an inner knowing, a sense of trust and wholeness. It's not that God told me I was going to make the Olympic team; it's that I felt a great peace about my future as a hurdler.

I remember getting up from that prayer feeling grateful and hopeful. I slept well that night, even though I still didn't have the answers. I think that's the kind of peace we are all looking for, the kind Jesus demonstrated when He slept on a boat in the middle of a storm (Mark 4:35–41).

The seas were raging, His disciples thought they were done for, and all the while, Jesus slept. I think He was able to sleep because His heart was at peace. Why? Because He knew His heavenly Father was bigger than the storm.

Of course it's true. God is bigger than every storm.

If you know the story, then you know that the terrified and

desperate disciples thought they were going to die, so they woke Jesus to save them. And Jesus, no doubt a little grumpy from being so rudely awakened, "rebuked the wind" and then said to the storm, "Peace, be still" (v. 39 KJV).

And the storm stopped raging.

THE FIX

The very next day, Dr. Bray found out what was wrong with me.

Apparently I was born with an incredibly rare birth defect. I'm special. Because I'm not a doctor, I'm going to hand the reins over to the professional.

Dr. Bray?

"It's called a tethered spinal cord. Her spinal cord was pinned down by a tail inside the middle of her nerves. She literally didn't know where her feet were, as she was losing the sensation in her feet. And it was causing her to fall."[3]

I was just not sharp. I was making errors that I normally wouldn't make, and I was in a lot of pain. But Dr. Bray performed the surgery to fix it.

"We did a microscope procedure on her to go inside the middle of the nerves and release her tethered cord."[4]

The surgery was a success, and so was the post-op anesthesia video of me that you can find online, if you're so inclined.[5] Or just keep reading.

In the video, I tell the *TMZ* reporter, "I'm seeing double right now. . . . I'm actually really disappointed because I requested double D implants at the same time. Clearly they did not honor that request, so those will have to wait. Really bummed about that."

The surgery and recovery are pretty technical, so I'll let Dr. Bray explain again.

Dr. Bray?

"This minimal incision just lets the athlete recover back to their potential."[6]

Okay, maybe not that technical.

I pretty much lived in a bed for the next month. My goal after the first month? Walk for twenty minutes a day.

It was a fast recovery, considering I had spinal surgery. But it was not easy. Before I could worry about being the fastest human in the world, I had to get back to doing normal things.

First, it was walking to the bathroom, then to the kitchen for water. Then I was strong enough to walk down the driveway and back, then to leave the house and go to the grocery store. It wasn't easy, and there were moments that really scared me.

I remember trying to walk down my driveway early on in my recovery. I got so overheated, I was sweating and exhausted, and by the time I reached the end of the driveway, I didn't think I could make it back to the house. My neighbors were at work, and I hadn't brought my phone, so I couldn't call anyone for help. I started to panic. I was worried I'd pass out in the hot Louisiana heat.

I thought that's how they were going to find me. All my years of competing and pushing my body through hard workouts, but in the end, I'd be known as the Olympian who couldn't make it down her driveway and back. It actually shook me up. I was in tears as I stood there for a good five minutes trying to calm my breathing. Eventually I was able to shuffle my way back up the driveway. Thinking about it now, I'm glad they held off on the breast augmentation.

I had the spinal surgery about a year before the 2012 Games, and I remember watching the world championships in the hospital. I saw the three girls run the hurdle race—one, two, three—and then get their medals. And I was like, "I'm in a hospital bed after having spinal surgery. How am I going to be one of the fastest runners in the world a year from now?"

VISUALIZATION AND MOVIE MONTAGES

If my life were a movie, this is where the training montage with inspiring music would be.

You've seen it. A Jamaican bobsledding team waking John Candy with "Rise and shine. It's butt-whipping time"; Daniel-son waxing on and waxing off in *The Karate Kid*; and, of course, Rocky Balboa drinking raw eggs before running through the blue-collar streets of Philadelphia while punching at the air. The horns start blowing rhythmically, and there's more running and push-ups and weight lifting and sit-ups and air punching and . . . oh, man, I love training montages.

None of those were me, though. For the first month after surgery, I could barely walk, which makes for a poor training montage. But I did start training to compete in the 2012 London Olympic 100-meter hurdles.

I was stuck in bed, so I had to use a new approach to training: visualization. There are studies on this. When athletes get injured, visualization helps them come back quicker.

There is a scripture about vision that I think is really helpful in understanding the value of visualization: "Where there is no vision, the people perish" (Proverbs 29:18 KJV). Another translation puts it this way: "Where there is no prophetic vision the people cast off restraint" (ESV). Visualization is actually about practicing that kind of restraint. In other words, if we don't have a clear picture of where we're going, it's easy to lose our way.

Amazingly, when done correctly, you can practice mental control over your body while lying down, and your body doesn't know the difference. It's all about repetition. It's crazy that even though you're not physically running over hurdles, even though you're not lifting a finger, your mind is empowered and conditions you mentally.

After my surgery, visualization became a core part of my training. I still practice it, especially in the fall through February, before the race season starts.

First, I lie on my back, normally on the carpet in my house.

Second, I take several deep breaths and slowly exhale until I feel all the tension leaving my body. Relaxed, I center myself in thankfulness.

Third, I visualize being on the track. I visualize the blocks, the hurdles, the finish line, the stadium, the noise, even the weather. I visualize sunny days, overcast days, and even rainy days. I visualize every scenario.

I visualize myself emotionally confident, knowing I am exactly where I need to be at this moment and appreciative of the fact that I can run.

Using all five senses, I immerse myself in the pre-race moment. I visualize taking off my warm-ups and then walking to the start line, feeling the track on my hands, putting my feet in the blocks, settling back into the blocks, like a spring ready to be sprung. My breathing is calm, controlled; my heart rate is steady. I am focused. It's the quiet before the storm, and everything is still.

Fourth, I visualize a slow-motion version of my race. The gun sounds, and I explode from the blocks. My first three steps are longer as I approach the first hurdle. I begin to quicken, then prepare to go over the hurdle and maintain my speed, making sure my body is in a good position. Then, as I get over the first hurdle, my arms tighten and everything just becomes an intense rhythm, to the point where I'm not even seeing the hurdles anymore. I just feel them.

I would often visualize so intensely at this point that the muscles in my thighs would be twitching and my legs would be moving as if I were actually hurdling. My body couldn't tell the difference between visualization and the real race.

Finally, I visualize finishing strong. The hurdles come fast, and I can see everything perfectly. I'm coaching myself as I clear every hurdle just by the smallest margin, and then I lunge at the tape.

Visualization helped me deal with anxiety after the surgery, when I was struggling to imagine how I was going to get from lying in bed to winning the gold medal in London in a span of twelve months.

It wasn't long before I was training again.

Coach Shaver had me going hard, running workouts in the mornings and doing Pilates, pool workouts, yoga, and rehab in the afternoons. Then I graduated to endurance-building runs and Death Valley, which is the name we gave to sprinting the stairs one, two, three at a time at LSU's football stadium.

I'd say now would be the time to start the training montage, except, well, it's rare to see athletes throwing up in montages, and I've thrown up in more seats in that stadium than I've sat in. Also, I was never able to lift up my hands at the top of the stairs to celebrate, like Rocky always does, because training for the Olympics isn't a montage; it's a brutal day-in-day-out obsession. And also there were no cameras.

Over the months I built up my endurance, until finally I was hurdling again and then competing again. But I was so behind, and every day was a fight. I wasn't running my best; I was getting a lot of 12.9- and 13-second times and doing a lot of losing. Every time I thought I was starting to make progress I'd hit a snag. Besides the surgery, I had two hamstring tears that year, both requiring extensive treatment.

There were a lot of moments when I didn't think I'd be ready in time. I was fighting a constant head battle. I was just trying to have faith and keep working.

I was praying and crying out to God every night; I felt so overwhelmed.

Near the beginning of the season, a journalist asked what I thought was the biggest threat to defending my 60-meter World Indoor title.

"Honestly, the biggest threat is me and my head," I said. "I'm coming off of one of the worst years I've had in my career. It can either really hurt your confidence or it can add fuel to the fire. So I am working hard to use it in a positive way, to motivate myself."[7]

At the end of the season I was motivated, but it wasn't the 60-meter indoor title I was focused on. That ship had sailed. Ready or not, I was focused on the London Olympics. And to reach that goal, I would have to qualify.

THE QUALIFYING ROUND

The Olympic trials take place in Eugene, Oregon, one month before the Games. There are three rounds: the qualifying round, the semis, and the finals.

You have to place in the top three to move on, and the top three finishes in the finals determine the Olympic hurdlers. Basically, if you don't at least place third in each race, you don't make the Olympic team.

In 2008, I was winning every race leading up to the Olympics. At the Olympic trials, I was undefeated in all three rounds and ran a 12.29 in the finals, which was the fastest time in the world that year. I was favored to win everything, and my confidence was leaps and bounds over what it had ever been.

It wasn't that way in 2012. Leading up to the Olympic trials, I was losing every race. It was so bad that I had to use a qualifying time from a 2011 race, because my times in 2012 weren't even fast enough to get me into the trials.

And my confidence? It was playing hide-and-seek with me, and I was having a terrible time trying to find it.

The commentators and track and field writers gave me little help. I was hearing statements like, "Her injury has set her back," "There is no way Lolo is making the Olympic team," and "It's over for her." All the predictors had me off the team and missing out on a chance to redeem 2008.

I placed third in the qualifying round.

Third. I ran a 13-second race!

It's called "by the skin of your teeth." I barely advanced and would need to place at least third in the next two competitive trials.

After the race I calmly and collectedly asked Coach Shaver a question. "Coach, I need you to stop lying to me. Like, do I look bad? . . . I mean, I feel good in the warm-up, and then I go out there and run thirteen seconds!"

Then I threw my shoe.

Okay, I actually had a screaming meltdown.[8]

My confidence was shaken. My mental toughness was under attack.

And then it rained.

THE SEMIS

The rainstorm seemed to come out of nowhere. One moment it was sunny; we were all stripped down, we'd done our warm-up, and we were literally lining up for the semifinals. And then all of a sudden the temperature dropped and the worst rainstorm exploded over our heads.

I think the officials didn't know what to do at that point. They didn't know whether to keep us there or not. They were probably thinking, *Maybe two minutes from now they'll be able to run*, or *Maybe we need to get them off the track and out of this weather.*

Meanwhile, we were standing under a downpour trying to stay warmed up to no avail.

It took what seemed like an eternity before they made the decision to call a delay. They ran us off the track and back into the call room.

Remember, this was the Olympic trials. This was not supposed to happen. We had been preparing for this race for four years. And the last year, for me, was the most brutal.

They took us back to the call room, but coaches aren't allowed in there.

At the Olympic trials, just like the Olympics, there's a process we all follow. First, we warm up with our coaches on the track outside. Then we go to the first check-in room or call room, leaving our coaches until after the race because they also aren't allowed on the track during the race. This is where the officials check our spikes, our bib numbers, and our uniform logos. Then we go to a second call room where we put on our spikes and do a few more drills on our own.

So typically there are about twenty to twenty-five minutes

where we don't have access to our coaches. No last-minute instructions. No last-minute calming of nerves. We're on our own.

In each of these call rooms, you sit with all your competitors, and you're nervous and your legs are twitching. Sometimes you're so nervous you feel nauseated, and like you can barely feel your hands and legs that you can't even tie your shoelaces. Sometimes you're doing three and four different knots on top, just to be sure. One year my spikes used Velcro instead of shoelaces, and that was a lifesaver.

You're sitting next to your competitors trying to remain focused, and it can play with your head. The call rooms can break athletes. Races have been lost in those rooms. The whole thing can cause you to mentally lose your game. It's pretty intense in there, and you have to know how to handle it.

That day of the semifinals it was still raining, and we were all in the second call room. At that point we had been away from our coaches for at least forty-five minutes, and everyone was trying to refocus because we had literally been lining up to race when the storm hit.

Most pro hurdlers have their coaches at every practice and every race. Their coaches rarely leave their side, and I could see other athletes cracking. The long stretch, the unusual race circumstances, the rain delay—it was all getting to them. They had too much time to think.

Suddenly I felt like I had an advantage.

First, because Coach Shaver is also a college coach and the end of the college season overlaps with the beginning of the pro season, I had competed many times without him at my race. So being without my coach wasn't impacting me like it was the other girls.

Second, I had seen this coming. You see, almost a year before I had started visualizing this day.

As I mentioned earlier in this chapter, I began practicing visualization in the late fall and continued with it through February, just before the season started. So in the call room, while I mentally prepared by thinking through techniques and execution, I suddenly felt a surge of confidence.

I had visualized every scenario for this race. I visualized being really nervous. I visualized that the hurdlers got out on me, and I had to come back. I visualized I was winning, and I had to stay sharp and focused. I visualized a sunny day, an overcast day, and even a rainy day.

I felt like I was in an invisible bubble. I wasn't thinking about anyone else or stressing over the circumstances. I was fine. I mentally didn't lose focus. I was still ready, and I was sharp.

After everything I had gone through that year—all my bad races, hamstring injuries, my spinal surgery—a rain hiccup was the least of my troubles.

I think God may have had something to do with that race, because we don't typically run on rainy days. But that whole year leading up to the Olympic trials, I had visualized going through my race motions on a wet track.

Eventually it stopped raining—and I came in second, this time under 13 seconds.

You'd think my confidence would be high at this point, right? It wasn't. The confidence I felt in the call room was suddenly hiding again.

Why? Because there are eight lanes in a hurdles race, and you earn your lane based on your last performance, your placement, and your time. And my second place time of 12.75 had me running in lane 2.

THE FINALS

In a hurdles race, you want a middle lane because you can get a better sense of the race there. When you're running in an outside lane, it's harder to get a feel for what's going on. You're just kind of running blind.

Because of my time in the qualifying round, I'd be running on an outside lane in the finals: lane 2. It meant I was projected to place last in the finals. It meant I was not expected to make it to the Olympics; I was expected to fail.

As I prepared for the race, I felt the weight of the last months settle on me. All the work, the pain, the sweat and tears, the terrifying days of not knowing what was wrong with me and wondering if my career was over, the really hard days of physical therapy and even harder days of rebuilding and retraining muscles—they had all led me to this moment: running in lane 2 against the best hurdlers in the United States.

I also felt the pressure that I would not be able to redeem myself from the 2008 Olympic "failure." That I would forever be known as the girl who hits hurdles.

Before the call rooms, during warm-ups, I remember trying to calm my doubts, fears, and nerves, visualizing a bit and aiming to have a strong heart to finish. I wasn't freaking out, just staying steady.

Then Coach Shaver gave me some advice just before I went into the final call rooms: "At the finish line, don't try to see your placement, don't glance left or right, don't worry about if you've made the team, don't focus on the results. Maintain your focus on straining and giving your all through the finish line."

Philippians 3:14 says, "I press on toward the goal to win the prize for which God has called me heavenward in Christ Jesus." My coach wanted me to press for the finish line and not focus on the prize.

And the advice landed.

It was what I needed to hear from the person I needed to hear it from, the person who had traveled these past thirteen years with me and knew the price I'd paid to be there.

His words further steadied and refocused me, because they reminded me of what I already knew to the very depths of my being. I was an experienced professional athlete, an Olympic hurdler. I put in the work. I was prepared. I was sharp, ready, and focused. I was mentally tough. I knew how to finish the race well.

You see, Coach Shaver helped me manage my emotions by reminding me to manage my focus. He reminded me of what I already knew to be true: I was ready.

I stood out on the track and relaxed my breathing. I took off my warm-ups, walked to the start line, felt the track on my hands, put my feet in the blocks, and settled back like a spring ready to be sprung.

Then I flinched.

WHEN YOU FLINCH

Before the race, in the call room, the officials made the announcement that they were not going to call false starts on flinches. I remember thinking, *No problem. I don't flinch.* I've never flinched in my whole life. Middle school, high school, college—I've never flinched in the blocks.

Flinching is when your body jumps a little bit as every muscle flexes in preparation to burst from the blocks, but then you catch yourself. Because your feet never leave the pads, it's not considered a false start. But it can be disastrous for the runner. The problem is, when you flinch, often you aren't reset when the gun sounds. That's what happened to me.

I was using every muscle to put on the brakes and reset as the gun was shooting off.

As runners were exploding forward, I was pulling back. A mistake like that in a 12-second race means it's over. Every hurdler knows this.

It's over, I thought.

Then I hauled arse.

That's the technical term.

I can remember every emotion and every stage of the 2008 finals. But the 2012 finals? I can't remember anything except panicked adrenaline.

After I crossed the line, I came back to myself.

It felt close, but honestly, I didn't know if I got third, fourth, fifth, or even sixth. That's how close the race was and how focused I was.

That moment, as I waited for my time and place, felt like an eternity. I was waiting with seven other girls to find out if my dreams were coming true or if they were crushed, if all the work I put in and all the pain and tears would be rewarded or if I'd watch the Olympics from my house.

I said a quick prayer and looked up.

Third place!

I had never been more thrilled about third place.

I got third in the first round, and then I made the Olympic team by placing third in the last round. By the skin of my teeth.

I was going to the Olympics again!

I can't explain my sense of joy and relief.

The crowd was going bonkers.

We took our victory lap.

It was my new and old Olympic teammates Kellie Wells and Dawn Harper and I again.

MENTAL TOUGHNESS AND OVERCOMING

On the track I was interviewed and asked how I felt. "It feels amazing. So many roadblocks and people counting me out, but I just kept overcoming. I'm thrilled and honored to represent everybody out there fighting for a dream."[9]

Overcoming is something you do on race day, but it's also the evidence of something you did every day before then. Overcoming is the fruit of hard work, the evidence you have good people around you, the proof of mental toughness.

You'll need mental toughness on race day. But it's only gonna be there for you if it's something you develop every day. You can't arrive at race day and then be mentally tough if you haven't spent time in Death Valley. And you'll need to surround yourself with people who can dodge shoes and still be there to remind you how mentally tough you actually are when you need to be reminded.

Mental toughness is what you practice when you can't walk, and so you lie in a bed and envision running. Mental toughness is developed in both losing and winning. If all you have ever done is win, you aren't mentally tough; you're just a good runner who has never faced adversity.

I think mental toughness is like faith. You develop it day in, day out through adversity, and then discover you have it when you find yourself suddenly in need of it. It's like peace. You can't really know if you have it until you're in a situation beyond your understanding, and suddenly there's peace.

We all have impossibilities in our lives, and the way we overcome them is through a mental toughness that has less to do with the moment and everything to do with the journey.

While I am no expert on faith and peace, I know a little about focus and visualizing and what it means to be on a journey in which every day is a grind. And in that grind is the opportunity to prepare for a breakthrough.

Mental toughness comes a few different ways. It comes when you mess up or can't get past something but then you eventually do and learn how to break through. It also comes as you gain confidence from having continued victories, from feeling untouchable.

You need a little bit of both, but too much of one or the other can throw you off. Even in my best seasons, when I'm winning races, I've had really low moments where I felt like I wasn't going to have a breakthrough. So I try to use it all. Use success, use failure—they all shape and cultivate you.

NEXT UP: LONDON AND THE DARK NIGHT OF THE SOUL

Dawn Harper congratulated me on the track, saying, "That was really impressive."

It felt sincere. She seemed happy for me, and I remember thinking, in the joy of the moment, that everything would be good this time. We were headed to the Olympics together once again, and maybe this time we were going to be all right.

We had both qualified for our second Olympics, a huge accomplishment, but once again, I found myself at the center of attention. After the race, much of the press attention was on the underdog: me.

As we got closer to the Olympics, and I continued to get more publicity, I think it reignited Dawn's anger from 2008. And in the days leading up to the 2012 Games, I began to sense it. That and the media backlash, plus feelings of resentment from my teammates, hit me in a way I had never experienced.

It led to the inquisition of Lolo Jones and the dark night of the soul.

TEN

THE INQUISITION OF LOLO JONES

After the Olympic finals, seasoned Olympic journalist Tim Layden wrote a piece about me for *Sports Illustrated*. He opened by saying, "She stood before inquisitors, largely ignoring the 1,500 behind her." He wrote briefly on my career—the highs, the lows, and specifically the tumultuous days leading up to the 2012 Games.

> Jones had come to London as arguably the most-publicized athlete on the U.S. Track and Field team. . . . This was in some part because of her accomplishments, as a two-time Olympian and, entering the Games, the fifth-fastest American woman in history. But in larger part, it was because in 2012, Lolo Jones was a story. She was a story first because she crashed into the ninth hurdle while favored and leading the Olympic final in Beijing. Then she was a story because she's attractive and landed on multiple magazine covers, backed up by stories about a genuinely challenging early life and a serious back surgery last summer that endangered

her career. Then she was a story because she announced on HBO that she will remain a virgin until marriage. And finally, she was a story because she got blowback about all those other things being oversold.

She then finished fourth in the fastest 100-meter hurdle race in Olympic history.[1]

Fourth.

I came in fourth at the 2012 Olympics.

Australian Sally Pearson won, setting an Olympic record. Second and third were my teammates, Dawn Harper and Kellie Wells.

FOURTH PLACE!

Coach Shaver has coached thousands of athletes and has encouraged many a disappointed "on the outside looking in" hurdler with a reflection on probability, giving them a perspective shift, if you will.

I had never heard this particular reflection from him directly, but I've known about it. So while writing this book, I asked him why I'd never been given the pep talk.

"Because with your ambition and drive and goals, it wouldn't mean anything," he said, and I was flattered.

But then I asked, "Maybe you can give it now, for the book?"

He nodded.

I tell kids in college, my athletes who qualified for an event but maybe didn't place, "Let's say there's over five hundred kids collegiately that are competing in the hurdles out there throughout the season. You know there's only gonna be eight finalists out of that five hundred people. There's only going to be eight people in the whole United States that are gonna make it.

"Well let's put that into perspective for a world championship or an Olympic Games. You're talking about thousands and thousands of athletes who are just trying to get there, you know? And of those thousands and thousands that are trying to get there, there's only thirty-two that make it. And of those thirty-two, there's only eight that are gonna make the final, and then there's only three that will medal. Of the thousands and thousands, there's only three that get medals."

You start putting it all into perspective, and I always say, "Dang, just getting there is awesome. Making a final is like a dream come true for everybody."

I nod. It's the truth. But he's also right that I have never needed to hear it before a race.

Coach Shaver kept going,

It doesn't mean that you shouldn't have that dream of medaling, but you're not any less successful being fourth than you would have been if you were third, or second, or even [won]. You did your very best and had one of your best performances of that particular season when it counted the very most.

Okay, I needed that.

I came in fourth. I lost out on medaling by a tenth of a second in what is still the fastest women's 100-meter hurdles final in Olympic history. What that means is that my time in any other Olympic race would have earned me a medal.

Coach Shaver's words reminded me of what he told me after the race—that even though I didn't have a medal, I was the winner of an invisible stat, a stat no one would really ever know but me. I was the first person to not medal in an Olympic Games with my race time. It frustrated me that I had that moment in history, but it also encouraged me, because I overcame insane odds to run in the fastest women's hurdle final in history.

Again, perspective is everything. My first reaction to fourth place was actually thankfulness. I had made the team. I had experienced God's overwhelming blessing. It was only by God's grace that I was there. A year earlier I'd had spinal surgery and wasn't even supposed to make the Olympic team.

You know, I felt like I had been in a brutal battle for a year and had accomplished so much. And then it was over. And I was like, *Oh my gosh, I got through that. I cannot believe I just got through all that, and I made it. I made it out alive.*

That was the 2012 season for me. I made it out alive.

Obviously I wanted to medal. I have never in my life run any race to get fourth. But in every Olympic race ever run, there has always been a fourth-best hurdler. And on that day, against all odds, I was that hurdler.

The fourth best.

In the world.

I have had days where I was the best hurdler in the world, and that's incredible. But every elite hurdler knows there's not much of a difference between the best in the world and the fourth best. We're talking a few tenths of a second.

So fourth best in the world on the world's largest stage? Are you serious? That's absolutely fantastic!

That was what I felt in the early hours after the race. But we don't live in a world that looks at the glass as half full, especially not in the world of professional sports. For so many, fourth place simply means "first-place loser."

And I knew that. I knew I would have to answer questions about what I had nearly won and therefore what I had lost. Again.

I wasn't naive. I was ready for the press to ask about being so close and missing out on medaling. What I wasn't ready for were what felt like the attacks, the mockery, and the hate. Especially from my teammates.

Not again.

It all started the next day and came at me hard and fast as I met with the press. While many were focused on what I had lost, many more wanted me to qualify myself as a legitimate contender, as though I hadn't deserved to be there in the first place.

These questions centered around whether I deserved the sponsorships I had been given now that the race was over, questions that had been raised by the press in the days leading up to this race.

This idea was being propagated both before and after the race by my own teammates. Kellie Wells, who placed third, was asked about me after the race, and she said, "I think that, on the podium tonight, the three girls that earned their spot, that got their medals, they worked hard and did what they needed to do, prevailed. And that's all that really needs to be said."[2]

It was such a belittling thing to hear, especially from a teammate, a fellow hurdler who knew the price we all paid to earn a chance to compete. So I didn't work hard enough? Is that what she was implying? That the girls who didn't win medals didn't work hard enough? After all my workouts, my pushing past rehab with tears, still, I didn't work hard enough and that's why I didn't win a medal?

You may be confused, wondering why a teammate would

question my legitimacy as a fellow competitor. Why would *Time* magazine publish an article after the race titled "Lolo Jones Finishes Fourth in the Olympics. So Did She Deserve to Be Heard?"[3]

The *Time* article ran because of another article that published two days before the race in which I had been viciously maligned by the *New York Times*.

EVERYTHING IS IMAGE?

Just before the Olympic finals, a writer by the name of Jeré Longman, who, evidence would suggest, is a self-righteous man who hides behind a veneer of journalistic integrity, wrote what I perceived to be a sexist hit piece on me for the *New York Times*.

It was nothing more than well-written contempt with a clever title: "For Lolo Jones, Everything Is Image." Journalists around the world quickly condemned the article as hypocritical and unfair, but not before the world read it.

It hurt. But I didn't pay it much mind before the race because, first, I'm an Olympic athlete who paid the highest of prices to be there and, second, it wasn't true.

However, after the race it had to be addressed because I was continually being asked about it, and worse, painfully so, my teammates had not only embraced the narrative but continued to promote it.

What was the narrative? I'll give it to you straight from Longman himself.

Jones has received far greater publicity than any other American track and field athlete competing in the London Games. This was based not on achievement but on her exotic beauty and on a sad and cynical marketing campaign. Essentially, Jones has decided she will be whatever anyone wants her to be—vixen, virgin, victim—to draw attention to herself and the many products she endorses.[4]

Longman, a man, determined that I, a woman, had "decided" to sell myself, in his words, as a "vixen, virgin, victim." Then he had the stones to write, "Women have struggled for decades to be appreciated as athletes."[5]

This guy literally attacked me under the guise of equality for women athletes as if I *wasn't* a woman athlete who had struggled for decades. He then went on to exploit my "exotic beauty" in order to question my convictions and professional accomplishments. The man attacked me for appearing on magazine covers as though he were exposing some great hypocrisy, as though I had revealed more skin on those covers, particularly the ESPN 2009 Body Issue, than is revealed in the top and bottoms I wear every time I clear a hurdle. He literally sexualized my body and then shamed *me* for what *he* had done.

You have to wonder if Longman also sexualizes the discus thrower. You know, the famous nude male Roman marble statue associated with the Olympics that can typically be found on display in the British Museum.

Longman couldn't seem to decide what argument he was making. Out of one side of his mouth he suggests I had sold my body to sponsors; out of the other side he suggests I didn't deserve the sponsorships.

A master manipulator of words, he next attacked my integrity as a Christian. If you read the article, you will quickly realize he doesn't actually care about equality for female Olympians or the broken Olympic system in which athletes struggle to financially support themselves. That was just the cover behind which Longman hid so he could express his seeming disdain for the fact that I am a Christian and a virgin and have been public about both. He seemed to be so offended by the idea of waiting to have sex until I was married that, in his condescension, he even lumped in Tim Tebow, the most famous face of abstinence before marriage at that time.

To support his misguided premise that my achievements didn't deserve the publicity I was getting, he quoted a well-intentioned director of the International Centre for Olympic Studies who said, "Limited opportunities are there for women to gain a foothold unless they sell themselves as sex kittens or virgins for sale."[6]

To me, it was a manipulation of a truth and a lie.

First, my virginity is not for sale, and shame on him for suggesting it is.

Second, Olympians are some of the poorest professional athletes in the world, and the best way we, male or female, hope to succeed is through sponsorships.

When it comes to sponsorships, Longman was partially right. Image does play a role in Olympic athletes getting the sponsorships needed to chase their dreams more successfully. The Olympic system is broken, and Longman noted it. But instead of addressing the real issue, the systemic greed within the US Olympic system and the lack of payment to hardworking and deserving athletes, he tarnished my image by suggesting I was the problem, as though I was on magazine covers because I was pretty instead of a hardworking, record-breaking, two-time Olympic athlete who had learned how to leverage her accomplishments and image so she could continue to chase her dreams within a broken system.

Third, and this is the big one, no one is given a spot on an Olympic team because he or she is good-looking. I don't care if you're a woman or a man, to even suggest it is the definition of sexist. I earned my way just like everyone else. If I happened to be receiving more publicity, it wasn't for lack of achievement.

I worked six days a week for twelve years to qualify for the London Games. Twelve years of breaking American and world records, winning and losing and winning again, often against Kellie and Dawn along the way. The prior year, I had overcome spinal surgery and two hamstring tears to earn an opportunity to represent the United States for a second time in the Summer Games.

And two days before I was to run, two days before I had the opportunity to finally earn a medal, a US newspaper released what I felt was some hack's sexist vitriol suggesting I was all about image.

Well, I don't know Longman, and though I hope he has since matured as a journalist and a human being, and though I've chosen to forgive him for what he wrote in 2012, consider this my official response: from beginning to end, his article was malicious BS.

And I am not alone in this opinion.

There was such journalistic and social media backlash to his article that a response was published by the *New York Times* editor. It wasn't a retraction as much as a weak defensive explanation. But even if it had been a retraction, it wouldn't have mattered. The damage was done.

The narrative of Lolo as vixen for sale, the hurdler who didn't deserve to be at the Games, still gets play even now. Longman's accusations hounded me for several years while I navigated what I believed was the betrayal of my teammates and fought to maintain a positive perspective on placing fourth.

But before I go there, I want to clear the air.

DAWN HARPER

I've wrestled with how to write about my history with Dawn. It's impossible to tell my story without telling some of hers. We are both such a huge part of each other's professional careers, and publicly so.

It's hard to explain how you overcame something and continue to heal from a particular pain without describing to some extent the nature of what hurt you. And Dawn hurt me. But I want to be fair to Dawn, because I know, along the way, she was also hurt.

Dawn is an incredible athlete and has made me better, simply because I had to run against her for so many years. We have both made each other better by winning against the other as the years passed.

Dawn has an amazing story. It's not mine to tell, but I feel I can at least quote the interview she gave to Michelle Beadle after she medaled in 2012.

> **Michelle Beadle:** You thought you weren't getting enough respect?
>
> **Dawn Harper:** I feel I had a pretty good story—knee surgery two months before the Olympic trials in 2008 to make the team [by] 0.007, [no] contract . . . working three jobs, living in a frat house, trying to make it work.

Coming off running in someone else's shoes [and] getting the gold medal.[7]

Dawn's story is truly inspirational. And it's actually crazy how much we had in common over the course of our careers, from not being able to afford shoes, to lack of sponsorships, to working multiple jobs so we could chase our dreams, to never quitting, to overcoming every obstacle so we could experience not just one but two Summer Games.

Dawn continued her interview with Michelle by talking about how in 2008 the press pushed her story aside for mine, and it hurt her feelings.

I get it. There's no doubt that in 2008 Dawn was disrespected by the press. Especially in the Matt Lauer interview I wrote about in chapter 7. She earned that gold medal, and Lauer shouldn't have juxtaposed her win against my loss. In my opinion, Longman did in his article what Lauer did in that interview: pit my teammates and me against each other.

Dawn and I have been used by the media to tell the story that gets the best ratings and best promotes the Olympics. The fact is, Dawn's story is inspiring. It should be told.

And not just Dawn's.

There is no Olympic story that isn't inspiring. Every Olympian has overcome crazy odds to be there. As Coach Shaver said, "'Of the thousands and thousands, there's only three that get medals.' You start putting it all into perspective and . . . 'Dang, just getting there is awesome.'"

That's what hurt most. Dawn knows the price an Olympic athlete pays, against all odds, to be there. And she knows I paid it.

But instead of defending me, instead of challenging the

Longman narrative, instead of being satisfied with the silver medal she earned and the accolades she was finally deservedly getting, instead of noting that every athlete has an incredible story, it felt like she dove headlong and was a full participant in attacking and maligning me.

FOURTH PLACE!

By the time I made it back to my room the night of the 2012 Olympic finals, and even more over the coming days and weeks, I lost the peace I briefly felt on the track after the race. That thankfulness and sense of accomplishment, that "just getting there is awesome" perspective was gone. I tried to turn the worship music on, I tried to praise, but I was pretty broken up and couldn't do it. I felt hard, angry, and bitter toward God.

I crumbled under the endless barrage from social media, the press, and my teammates as they attacked my worth as an athlete, an Olympian, a woman, a Christian. They mocked my athletic ability as well as my virginity. Some were actually saying that if I'd had sex, I would have won a medal. Dumb stuff, I know. But it landed. My Twitter blew up with comments like "You should give all your endorsements back, you're a flop" and "You couldn't medal, again," followed by laughing emojis.

With each article and comment my bitterness grew.

Where was God?

In 2008, when I was on the track, I heard, *But you're here*, and there was a sense of peace that followed me into my room, where I worshiped and praised and trusted. And that peace followed me into the days and weeks and years to come.

In 2012, after an initial sense of peace on the track, I couldn't regain it. My bitterness turned to anger. I took it out on God. I felt like He had allowed people to mock me. Why didn't He protect me better?

I know. This is when you ask why I was reading articles and checking Twitter. It's a popular thing for athletes to say, "I don't do social media" or "I don't read the press." But it's not true. We all read the press, including me, especially because part of our income is connected to sponsorships. Whether I like it or not, my image matters to sponsors. It was also impossible to avoid hearing comments when everywhere I went, people were noting what I had missed instead of what I had gotten.

I couldn't believe it myself—fourth place! *Are You kidding, God?*

On the track I had a good perspective on fourth place, a healthy view of what I'd accomplished. But for many, many days afterward, I was beaten down by a very different perspective.

The fourth-best NFL or NBA player is amazing, right? But fourth place in track and field is simply the first person not to medal. Mentally, fourth is the hardest placement, because it's always about not making the top three instead of what you've accomplished. Even more so if you're an American, because the United States is so good at the Summer Games. We almost always win the medal count. So fourth is like, "Oh, so you didn't medal?"

In the years since the 2012 Olympics, after hearing where I placed, no one has ever said, "Oh my gosh, you got fourth! That's amazing!"

No, it's always an apologetic look of commiseration. "Oh, so close!"

It's actually easier to place fifth through seventh, because then the response is, "Wow, that's so good!"

I'm writing about perspective again, right?

And, admittedly, my perspective shifted from what I had

accomplished to what I had lost. I was so deeply disappointed at losing out on a medal, which makes sense. But on top of that, I couldn't shake the sense of betrayal I felt from my teammates and what felt like an endless stream of mockery from the press and the public.

After the Games, I went home and sat on my couch for a month in a depressed state. I didn't really know what to do. I knew I didn't want to run; my heart hurt just thinking about it. I watched a lot of TV and cried out to God, venting my disappointment and anger.

I was at the lowest of lows. It felt as if all the progress I had made in the 2012 season, all the years I had pushed myself, had come to nothing. During those dark days, my story, the one I internalized, had somehow been reduced to loss.

I was drowning in bitterness.

I didn't know what step to take next.

But I knew I had to take one.

A NEXT STEP AND THEN ANOTHER AND ANOTHER . . .

Bitterness is a cancer. It slowly kills everything: hope, trust, your future. I knew this. But as G.I. Joe says, "Knowing is half the battle."

The other half? Well, I had to do something.

Have you ever seen the movie *Cool Runnings*? It's a classic. I grew up on this movie, and during that month on the couch, miserable and lost, I watched it again. If you haven't seen it, you really should. It's John Candy at his best, coaching a Jamaican bobsled team to the Winter Games.

While track and field was too painful a pursuit directly after

2012, I still had a desire to compete. And I knew that if I still had the fire, life wasn't over.

So I decided, "You know what? I'm gonna become a bobsledder. It's perfect. The press will leave me alone, I can step away from some of the pressures and disappointments I feel stuck under, and I can get out of the Louisiana heat. Yeah, I'm gonna be a bobsledder. Maybe even an Olympic one."

Okay, that's not the whole story, but it's closer than you'd think. I'll give you the rest in the next chapter. I also wasn't kidding about *Cool Runnings*—it's awesome, and you should watch it. And what I said about what to do when you feel stuck? I meant that too. Do *something*. Take a step.

My bobsled goal got me off the couch and focused on something other than my bitter disappointment after the 2012 Games. But as I dove headlong into this new snow-covered adventure, I knew I would have to take some other steps as well, steps for the sake of my heart.

While it was good to have something to throw myself into, I knew bitterness is a heart condition that, if left unchecked, can slowly destroy my future. I knew I had some heart work to do. To be honest, if you want to live life to its fullest, free of envy or bitterness, you will always have heart work to do.

I'd love to tell you about some magical prayer I've discovered along the way that fixes everything, that heals deep disappointment and frees you from bitterness. But if there is such a prayer, I haven't found it. What I do know is the principle I've been writing about for ten chapters now: have faith and do the work.

Faith starts with trusting in the goodness of God, even if you're mad at Him.

Long ago I decided that God gets the credit for all my victories and none of the blame for my defeats. While I might not have described it this way at the time, having faith is making the choice to believe that God is good and always there for me, regardless of my circumstances, disappointments, or ability to understand.

I know, your head is probably saying, "That doesn't make sense." But I bet your heart knows the truth. I think it's a good way to describe faith. And I think, because I believe it to the core of my being, even when I don't feel it, even when I am angry at God, even in my darkest moments, the dark night of the soul, there has been grace to trust God and go to work.

To take the next step.

When it came to bitterness, my next step was, in a word, thankfulness. Once again, I had to shift my perspective. I couldn't find a way to thank God for fourth place, but I could thank Him for His provision, in particular, financially. And it helped to soften my heart.

I also discovered I needed to take another step to deal with my bitterness. I needed to forgive. This one has been harder for me. You can know something is right and good for you yet still not feel it. And forgiveness has been one of those things. But I have a will, and I can make decisions with it.

In the years since 2012, I have chosen to forgive those who hurt me. And most days I succeed at it, although I haven't perfected it. I don't always feel it, but there's still time, and I'm putting in the work.

By the way, forgiveness doesn't mean forget. It doesn't mean I can't be honest about what I experienced. It just means I can be set free from the bitterness that is always birthed in unforgiveness.

It's another step forward. Another way to express my faith. Another way to trust God.

While the sting of those dark days still visits me, I continue to take steps. And the fact is, if we aren't taking steps, we're stuck.

I want to tell you, over the last several years, most days I have been able to regain a healthy perspective. I can once again see 2012 the way Coach Shaver does: "Just getting there is awesome. Making a final is like a dream come true."

I still want an Olympic medal. But the good news is, even if I never get one, I know I'll be okay.

FOURTH PLACE!

In 2016, the anchors of *CBS This Morning* asked what I would say to my critics, the haters on the internet who say, "She ain't won no medals."

I said, "I can tell them my stats, I can tell them I'm a three-time world champion, I can tell them I'm the fastest American indoor record holder . . . [but] that means nothing to them. At the end of the day, I just have to know that my opinions of what I've done on the track [are] not altered by what they think of me."[8]

I went on to talk about how anyone who chases their dreams will face criticism. Anyone who pursues a goal, whether it's starting a business, getting further education, or losing weight, will face haters and naysayers. But take joy in the victories along the way and learn from the defeats.

There's a quote from *Cool Runnings* when Jamaica enters their first bobsled team in the Winter Games. John Candy's character tells one of the bobsledders, "A gold medal is a wonderful thing. But if you're not enough without one, you'll never be enough with one."[9]

It's true. Even if you don't have your dreams, you need to know your worth, or else, once you have your dreams, they will still seem empty.

The fact is, you will win and you will lose, but you will grow the most through the losses. The races I've lost are where I have grown the most, where I have learned how to persevere, to press on, to trust God, to not give up, to take another step. I've learned that the haters don't get a say in interpreting my story, nor can they take from me what, by the grace of God, I have accomplished.

So practice thankfulness and forgiveness and get your perspective right!

Because there has always been a fourth-best hurdler. And in 2012, against all odds, on the largest stage, I was the fourth-best hurdler.

In the world.

ELEVEN

WIN OR LOSE, I'LL PRAISE HIM

There's a saying in bobsled competition: "Any run you don't use your helmet is a good run."

In other words, any run where you don't crash is a good run.

Yeah, I joined a sport where I need a helmet to protect myself from the possibility of death.

There aren't many similarities between bobsledding and hurdles. Yes, both sports use a track and there's a run, but that's just wordplay. The bobsled "track" is a narrow, twisting, banked slide made of ice, and the "run" is done while sitting in a gravity-powered, four-hundred-pound bullet-style sled that shoots down the track at speeds of up to ninety miles per hour.

For both sports, though, the fastest time wins. Once again, I was in a sport where winning and losing are measured by hundredths of seconds.

One more similarity: we start by running. We push the sled for the first twenty-five feet or so before jumping in. This part of the race is why, over the last several decades, a handful of track and field athletes have joined bobsled teams. Power and speed are pretty important at the beginning of a bobsled run; start times play a large role in finish times. That's why I was invited to compete for a spot on Team USA and to try out for the 2014 Sochi Olympics.

So, after the heartbreak of 2012, I turned my attention to bobsledding. There were two reasons I thought I could do this. First, the classic, incredibly inspiring movie *Cool Runnings*. (If you haven't watched it by now, just put the book down. Seriously, dog-ear the corner and go watch the movie. I'll wait.)

Second, for many years I trained with a Canadian track and field team that former LSU track and field athlete Glenroy Gilbert coached. Gilbert is a great guy. He competed in the Summer Games and then famously changed sports and joined the US bobsled team to compete in the Winter Games.

I never talked with him about it, but because of his connections with LSU, every year at the beginning of the track and field season, his team would come down and train with us. And I would be presented with the idea that if I ever found myself fighting deep depression after an Olympics, I could take a break from track and field and become a professional bobsledder.

What I am trying to say is, seeds were planted—first by my childhood infatuation with *Cool Runnings*, and then by a man who had shown me what was possible.

Just a quick note: pay attention to seeds. God often plants them, and if you water them, well, impossibilities become possibilities.

BOBSLEDDING

There are a couple things I should explain about bobsledding.

First, it got its name from a guy named Bob, who had a sled and knew how to use it. Yeah, that's not true. Fun fact: "The sport earned its name after competitors adopted the technique of bobbing back and forth to increase the speed of the sled."[1]

Second, I was part of a two-woman bobsled team: the pilot and, me, the brakeman. The pilot sits in front and pilots, which is highly technical and takes years of practice, dedication, and absolutely no bobbing. The brakeman sits in the back and provides weight, prayers, and encouraging thoughts. They could also be encouraging words, but the pilot wouldn't be able to hear them, as the noise inside a bobsled has the decibel level of a jet engine. So unless you're screaming at the top of your lungs, it's pointless.

My job, and the reason a track athlete—who, by the way, hadn't been sledding since she transformed a cardboard box into a snow sled during her childhood in Des Moines, Iowa—could compete for a spot on an Olympic team, was to provide power off the start line. I was the engine. Because of the years I committed to perfecting my burst off the blocks, I was an ideal candidate for the position of bobsled brakeman.

But a brakeman has a second job, which also does not include bobbing. At the end of the race, after providing a good push at the beginning of the race, my job was, you guessed it, to pull the brakes.

That's why they call us the brakemen.

THE BEST SPORT EVER

Lake Placid is a beautiful small town in the Adirondack Mountains of Upstate New York. It's like a Hallmark Christmas movie, like something you would see in a snow globe. It's one street, a handful of restaurants, and the Olympic Training Center. And for a season, it became home. And I loved it.

While I had started training in Louisiana, I continued in earnest once I arrived in New York.

What's training like? Well, have you ever heard of bobsled booty? It would be odd if you had, because it's an inside joke referencing the glutes of an Olympic bobsled athlete. Yeah, lots of lower body. Bobsledding is all about the ability to push something, and that means glutes, hips, thighs, and calves.

It also means gaining weight.

As a hurdler, I am 130 pounds shredded. My focus is to be light, agile, fast, flexible, and dynamic. In bobsledding, I had to put on 25 pounds so I could push a 365-pound sled.

I also had to put on weight because bobsledding is a gravity sport and "mass pushes mass." That's not just a bobsled principle; that's science. The maximum combined weight allowed for two women and a bobsled is 750 pounds. And we did our best to get as close to the max weight as possible.

What did that mean for Lolo Jones?

Ice cream every day. Sometimes even twice a day. Ice cream was literally part of my training! When bobsled athletes eat dinner, you might hear them say, "Doing it for gravity."

The Olympic Training Center provided all our meals for free. I remember the first time I went in they had two big buckets of ice cream. At first I thought it was crazy. I was like, "Why is there ice cream at the Olympic Training Center?" It just seemed like the most counterintuitive thing in the world.

But I got used to it. And I never got tired of it, because they changed the flavors every day. I don't know if you're getting this, so allow me to repeat it: *different flavors every day!* The best were the mint chocolate chip and praline days. But, you know, I like all the flavors.

And it wasn't just ice cream.

While I learned later that there are healthier ways to gain weight, for that first bobsled team, I kinda approached it like a college student. Which is a good way to describe that season of my life. Everything was set up like a college: dorm-style rooms, cafeterias, and lots of single people all in the same season of life with a similar focus on working hard, hanging out, and eating whatever they wanted.

I had pizza and bacon double cheeseburgers and fries and milkshakes and protein shakes with whipping cream.

And wings.

I would have wings while training for track, but track athletes typically give themselves only one cheat meal a week. I would wait until Tuesday, because Tuesday was half-price wings day. I started that tradition when I was driving my scooter back and forth to Home Depot, but I stuck with it even after I started getting contracts.

But in bobsled, I could have wings on Tuesday *and* every other day of the week. I could even have them twice a day if I wanted, or more specifically, for my second dinner, the meal right after I had the bacon double cheeseburger or chicken alfredo.

Before I go any further, I want to weigh in on the great wing-dipping debate between blue cheese versus ranch: blue cheese is disgusting.

It was surreal that I could have a second dinner around ten o'clock at night. But even though the food at the Olympic Training Center was free for breakfast, lunch, and dinner, dinner stopped at eight o'clock. So that's how I discovered my favorite restaurant, Wiseguys. It's where all the athletes went, partly because there weren't really any other options and partly because they had the best wings.

This was the college experience I'd never had when I was in college. At LSU, as a track athlete on a scholarship, at ten o'clock I was alone, hungry, and in bed. At ten o'clock as a bobsledder, I was at Wiseguys with my teammates having a second dinner.

And I was like, *This is the best sport ever.*

A TEAMMATE AND HEALING

Those early bobsled days were incredibly healing for me. While God and I didn't talk as much, since I was still raw with disappointment and hurt, I was thankful to Him for the new opportunity. In 2012, my faith had been rattled. But now I could sense my faith growing.

Bobsledding was a gift from God. It was a season where I didn't feel the daily pressure to be the face of the Christian athlete or defend my principles or disprove false narratives about being image focused or justify myself as a professional athlete to the press and social media or listen to another person commiserate about fourth place and the fact that I didn't have a medal. No, I was just Lolo Jones, an Olympic hurdler trying to make an Olympic bobsled team.

That came with a ton of pressure, of course. But it was the kind of pressure I love, the kind I thrive under; it was the pressure of authentic competition.

Bobsledding provided more than a reprieve from disappointment. I was finally experiencing what it was like to be on a team.

In bobsled I was suddenly and truly on a team. It surprised me how much I loved it, how much I needed it. Not that there wasn't drama. Competition brings out the best and worst in people. But in those early days, I discovered what it was like for a teammate to have my back and vice versa, and it was healing. God was very much working on my heart.

Actually, the Olympic bobsled is a team within a team. There are three Team USA sleds, each with a pilot and a brakeman. And they are numbered USA-1 through USA-3, in order of statistics and expectations. All three teams compete for medals against countries like Germany and Canada, but also against each other. So I was on a team within a team.

I made USA-3. And *we* earned it.

"We" is me and my pilot, teammate, and friend Jazmine Fenlator. Jaz beat out other pilots and I beat out other brakemen to make the team, and we did it together.

For months leading up to the Games, pilots and brakemen are mixed and matched like socks as the coaches and pilots look for the perfect fit. The coaches and pilots want the right pairings, and they have several measurables to make their decisions, such as which combination of pilot and brakeman can provide the best push time, velocity, and downtime.

But unlike track, which is cut and dried with the best three times going to the Games, the bobsled teams are ultimately determined by the coaches, and include not only some measurables but also some variables that are subjective, such as "She pushes great, but for some reason the pilot only gets fourth place with this brakeman," or "We want that pilot, but she doesn't like _____ brakeman, so that brakeman is out."

In the months leading up to the Games, I competed like I always have. I worked hard and, in this case, learned fast. But there was a new dynamic that was subjective, because it had to do with compatibility.

Pilots are the rock stars of the bobsled world. They have a huge say on who their brakeman will ultimately be, and while looking for the perfect pairing, they often trade brakemen out like, well, old socks.

It was competition, and I knew how to compete. But this

subjective aspect of the competition was new for me. For instance, one day I was pushing with Elana Meyers, an Olympic medalist, and the next day I was pushing for a pilot who just got her braces off. That wasn't an insult; everyone there was elite. But finding that pairing, that perfect two-woman team, is an important part of a successful bobsled run.

When Jazmine and I connected, it was amazing, both on the bobsled track and off. Jaz will be at my wedding one day, probably as a bridesmaid, but I haven't told her yet.

Jazmine became my pilot. I would fight, die, kill, steal, or whatever I needed to do for her, and vice versa. I was there to make her great, and she was there to do the same for me.

There's something powerful about teamwork when it's partnered with friendship. It's good for your soul, but it's also good for your downtime. Jazmine and I were a good team and good friends. We really enjoyed each other's company. In competitions, you room with your pilot. And we used to stay up way too late laughing at the dumbest stuff.

You can definitely have a teammate who isn't a friend. I've seen it. But that wasn't Jaz and me.

Teammates are there for each other; their job is to build each other up. Jaz was the best at this. I learned a lot from her, and I found a lot of healing through our friendship.

Jaz saw me for who I was. She saw all the hate I got from the track world, and she built me up. She called out jealousy, she spoke to my ability, and she praised my work ethic. "You're amazing, a beast" are the things you want to hear from your teammate, especially when you are new to the sport, and Jaz was good at giving them.

The fact is, Jazmine could have seen my inexperience as a

disadvantage for her chances at making the Olympic team, but she didn't. She believed in me.

And I believed in her. She was a newer pilot competing for her first opportunity to represent the United States, and she was a fighter. She was a really good driver working to develop more power in the start. She worked harder than the person next to her, so you could never count her out or overlook her. And I told her this.

I also told her she didn't crash me as much as the other drivers were crashing their brakemen. So, yeah, in my book, that made her a good pilot.

CRASHING

Bobsledding is really dangerous.

Sometimes, while traveling at extreme speeds, the bobsled crashes. Actually, the pilot crashes it. That's the way we brakemen put it because, let's face it, we're not the ones steering.

There is another big saying in bobsled: "You are not really a bobsled athlete until you have had your first crash." So, yeah, I am now a real bobsledder.

Every track is different in bobsled. They are shorter and longer, faster and slower. Sometimes you're in the bobsled for forty-five seconds, sometimes over a minute.

The severity of a crash depends on where you are on the track when you crash. At the top, with sixteen curves to go, you're in for a hellacious experience of twists and turns and screaming. At the bottom, well, it sucks too. I'm being lighthearted, but it can be terrifying.

When a bobsled crashes, it flips, often more than once. When the bobsled is upright, you feel the wind on your back. When it flips over, your back is now on the ice. And if your back is on the ice too long, you get ice burns. You literally can feel your skin melting. It happens very quickly, is incredibly painful, and leaves some of the nastiest scars.

We do wear burn vests, but they don't save you for that long. You have about five seconds before you have to make a calculated decision: eject or ride it out and risk getting burned. And this has to be decided while the bobsled is flipping, while you're disoriented, while you're getting thrown around, while you're gripping the parallel side rails to keep yourself in the sled as gravity's g-forces are trying to suck you out.

Most of the time you're safer inside the sled. Ejecting comes with the risk of catching your leg on part of a curve or snagging the spikes you used at the top to push yourself across the ice that could now catch in the ice and snap your ankle.

I've seen it. It's brutal and potentially career ending. So you have to make the right decision when you crash.

The sound of that flipped bobsled roaring down the track is the most frightening thing. It's like being in a violent car crash, except there are no seat belts, airbags, or safety features.

I remember my first crash on an easy track in Winterberg, Germany. Jazmine crashed me at the end of a practice run. I'd heard the horror stories, way worse than what I just described, so I was ready for the worst. Looking back, it was snowing that day, so the track wasn't as fast, and neither was the crash. I remember laughing and saying, "That's it? That's what you guys have all been warning me about? I've had harder falls when I hit hurdles and fell on the track!"

A few weeks later I ate my words. Jaz crashed me on one of the hardest tracks in Königssee, Germany, and it was the most horrifying experience of my life. She crashed me at the top, a part of the track called the S-curve. We still had most of the track left: curve after curve after curve, with no straightaway to get out. And the bobsled kept flipping. I got thrown around like a rag doll and couldn't eject because of the curves and the continuous flipping. I was stuck in a barrel roll.

I remember screaming. It was the loudest scream of my life. It was so bloodcurdling that I couldn't believe it was coming from me. And Jaz confirmed it. She said it was worse than anything she had ever heard and was frightened for me. But it turned out okay. I mean, I need to figure out where to send my therapy bill, but otherwise I'm okay.

That was the last run of the day for us. But the next day we were back at it. Within a few days, I could tell the story without shaking. And eventually with even a little humor, which was about the time Jazmine started adding how she was scared not just for me but also for herself, because when I was screaming, she thought, *Oh crap, I just crashed one of the most popular athletes in the world.*

FREEDOM

When I joined the bobsled team, my fellow teammates knew who I was. Or at least they knew what the papers had written about me. Each teammate had to come to her own conclusion about whether I was a beloved Olympic athlete or a vixen focused on my own publicity. And I did all I could to be me, Lolo Jones, an athlete competing for a spot on the team.

Brakemen aren't typically interviewed by the press; it's all about the pilot. But because of the 2012 publicity, I got more attention than normal. I laid low, and for a while I enjoyed a little anonymity. And whenever the cameras did show up, I made sure to put my teammates in the spotlight.

After Jazmine and I made the Olympic bobsled team of USA-3, the *Today* show wanted to interview me. I told my agent, "I'm not doing an interview unless they put all my teammates on there: the three pilots and the three brakemen."

I also used my social media to focus on my teammates. I did anything I could to shine a light on the US team as well as to preemptively diffuse any attention that might resurrect or add fuel to the 2012 narrative. I admit, I was fragile. I didn't want to experience that pain again. I just wanted a chance to prove myself.

But when some of the brakemen who didn't make the Olympic team were interviewed, they suggested I had made the team because of my popularity. I get it. The narrative was out there, and they knew about it. I also get that we all work so hard to make an Olympic team, and the pressures of competition are so great in our lives, that when disappointment strikes, when we can't understand, we look for a reason, anything to make sense of our circumstances. And when we're disappointed, we can lash out. I've been guilty of it myself.

That's all it took. The press ran with it. Many media outlets simply retooled and reposted their 2012 articles. It was the same story, just a new sport: Lolo made the Olympic bobsled team not because of her athletic achievement but because of her popularity and looks.

It hit me hard, and I was like, *God, please, not again.* I felt the weight of disappointment hovering like a dark cloud waiting to crash in and undermine my peace, joy, and sense of self. And for a moment I felt utterly alone. But I said nothing to the media. I thought I'd just ride it out.

Then something amazing happened. My teammates had my

back. Elana Meyers, the pilot of USA-1, upset at what was being written about me, responded with a post on her Facebook page defending me. Jazmine came to my defense too, letting everyone know I was her brakeman, and she continued to encourage me.

Even Darrin Steele, the CEO of USA Bobsled at the time, defended me, telling the Associated Press that the competition was "incredibly close" between me and the other girls who were excellent athletes, but that I had "absolutely" earned a spot on the Olympic bobsled team.[2]

While it didn't matter to the press, and they continued to carry on with their narrative, it mattered to me. It meant the world to me that my teammates, especially Jazmine, had my back.

We went to Sochi and competed our butts off. I was thankful, full of faith and joy and life. The experience was amazing.

We placed tenth, Jaz and me. And I think we were happier than some of the athletes who medaled. That's how strong our bond was.

Don't get me wrong. Everything in me wanted a medal. But my prayer has always been, "If we win, we praise Him, and if we lose, we praise Him." I've prayed that prayer before so many races, and that was my heart going into Sochi. I was thankful for my teammates and the opportunity to compete. That bobsled season was powerfully healing, and my friendship with Jazmine was better than a medal.

If you have read this far, you know that's a strong statement.

It's a true statement, but it's really hard to write.

I am a competitor. I compete to win. And yet I am continuously learning that life is not about winning and losing. It's about the peace and joy I possess while winning and losing. It's about the friendships and trust I've built while winning and losing.

I have often wondered which I would choose if the devil offered me a deal. "You can be paired with Jaz and place tenth, or you can be paired with another pilot and medal. But if you choose that option, you and Jaz are going to hate each other for the rest of your lives."

The answer is Jazmine. But it's not an easy answer.

I mean, I do cherish Jaz, but she knows how long I've been pushing for a medal.

CHASING A DREAM

I have been chasing an Olympic medal for twenty years. But not just a medal. I have been chasing the respect that comes with it.

As an athlete, I am measured and valued by my performance. There's so much I love about this. But when it comes to life, there is nothing more unsettling, devastating, and insecurity inducing than being measured by your performance and, regardless of your accomplishment, being found wanting—or worse, being betrayed by your teammates.

For twenty years I have looked to earn the respect of my peers from the world of track and field, while fighting the great insecurity that comes from somehow not measuring up in their eyes.

What I've learned, ultimately, is that respect is an inside job.

Over those twenty years I have had to learn how to chase a dream while not letting that dream define my identity, my sense of self-worth.

My story isn't over, but as of writing this, I haven't medaled in the Olympics. It's possible I never will.

And it's painful.

I have put in the work and given so much of my life in the pursuit of an Olympic medal. This pain is connected to authentic disappointment. It's about loss. It's a place where I have had to grow in faith—learning that, win or lose, I'll praise Him and trust in His goodness regardless of the outcome.

Another pain is connected to my identity. This pain is birthed from believing the lie that says, "You aren't enough *until*, you haven't arrived *until*, you won't be happy *until*, you won't know peace *until*, you won't experience respect from others or from yourself *until*, you won't know life, love, wholeness *until you medal*."

Until, until, until . . .

This second experience of pain is sneaky and deceitful, because it suggests that my identity is tied to something outside of Christ, outside the love of God, outside a belief in my own self-worth. It comes from believing the lie that medaling will be what truly, finally fulfills, secures, and settles me. As though a medal will make me a better person and give me true peace and sustaining joy, or as Jesus calls it, "life . . . to the full" (John 10:10).

I love competition, the simplicity of performance. But it has no place in my identity. I am learning to recognize the lie that attaches my identity to my performance.

A lie is defeated once you embrace the truth. And the truth is, my identity is secured in Christ, not in what I have or haven't achieved. It's not about what I have done; it's about what Jesus already did on the cross. It's about the trust Jesus placed in His heavenly Father when He said, "Into your hands I commit my spirit" (Luke 23:46). In other words, "Win or lose, I will praise You."

Here is what I know: If respect, peace, joy, and sense of fulfillment are determined by our achievements, we are climbing a mountain that can never be summited. We are inviting a lifetime of heartache.

I think life is about more than arriving at our desired destination. Life is a series of wins and losses and not quitting along the way. It's about learning how to thrive regardless of whether you medal, come in fourth, or even tenth.

Life is about faith. It's about learning how to trust God and good people.

Life is about hurdling disappointment. It's about thankfulness, perspective, friendship, and living generously. It's about trust. It's about celebrating the wins and learning from the losses. It's about competing your arse off and then trusting God with the outcome.

WIN OR LOSE, I'LL PRAISE HIM

The pressure of competition has often revealed what I believe about God, myself, and others. Competition is a powerful thing. It can both develop and reveal character. It's like a mirror. It doesn't lie; it exposes everything, good and bad.

Do you have the grit and work ethic to compete and win? Do you also have integrity and generosity and confidence when you lose? You can decide if you're going to play the petty game of insecurity or the honorable game of confidence in God and self.

We live in a world that is all about competition, all about winning and losing. But the question in life and faith isn't about that; it's about whether or not we can be people of character and kindness, regardless of winning or losing. Can we live confidently in our identity? Can we access peace and joy even when the circumstances suggest both to be foolish? Can we trust God?

At times I have broken under the pressure of competition and haven't liked what it revealed. At other times I have thrived under the pressure of competition and discovered God's grace.

Bobsledding has been a reprieve and a joy, a new challenge. I built some lifelong relationships there; I experienced an authentic team. I've also seen its ugly side. Sometimes I have thrived, and sometimes I've failed.

But I continue to compete, professionally and in life, to attack and clear hurdles, and to trust God. I continue to become the best version of myself. I continue to experience success. I continue to discover my identity is in Christ.

We live in a world that is performance focused. And I am learning how to be in this world but live for another. I am learning how to live in Christ, and then, regardless of the attacks from the media or teammates, to know joy and peace.

I am learning that whether I am wrongfully accused or disrespected, whether I feel weak or not good enough, whether I am struggling with poverty and driving a scooter to work, whether I am faced with inequality, whether I am still single, whether I haven't medaled, whether my disappointment is profoundly felt, my identity is sure and I can trust God.

I am truly learning, "If I win, I'll praise Him, and if I lose, I'll praise Him."

And you know, that's really good.

TWELVE

TWELVE-SECOND PERFECTION

Twelve seconds is a significant measurement of time for me. There aren't many things that can be accomplished in that time. Yet I've spent most of my life chasing the perfect 12 seconds. It just seemed wrong to have a book with only eleven chapters. So I added a chapter you should be able to read in the time it takes me to clear ten hurdles.

AFTERWORD

*Everyone loses. Everyone comes up short. Winners are
talented, but most winners are just losers that never gave up.*

—LOLO JONES, INSTAGRAM

God is funny, you know? I never thought I'd go back to Beijing. I've
purposely avoided going back. There have been many opportunities for me to return and run races, but I haven't.

But the 2022 Winter Games are in Beijing. The Winter and
Summer Games have never been in the same city in the history of
the Olympics until now. And it feels like a God thing, an opportunity.
Here's how the Associated Press put it:

> Lolo Jones hasn't returned to China since 2008, since one
> bad step in what was then the biggest race of her life cost her an
> Olympic gold medal.
>
> She's never wanted to go back.
>
> Her stance might change in 2022.
>
> Jones—the longtime U.S. hurdles star who decided to add
> sliding to her resume a few years ago—is back with USA Bobsled,

making this season's 10-woman national team as a push athlete. That puts her squarely in the mix for the next Olympics, which just happens to be in Beijing, the city where that misstep in the 100m hurdles final happened 12 years ago.[1]

My warm-up for the 100-meter hurdles is a lap around the oval track. In track we begin the race on the start line and run one whole lap to finish back where we started.

Finishing where I started feels like a great way to end my Olympic career.

If I make this Winter Olympic team—and I've got a good shot of doing so—I will get an opportunity to face my fears and show people that one mistake doesn't break you.

It's also an opportunity to fix something.

In 2008, before the race, I didn't pray to win a medal; I prayed that I would inspire. Working to make the Beijing Olympic bobsled team feels like God is continuing to answer that prayer. Except maybe this time I can win a medal as well.

My prayer isn't different for this opportunity, but I am different. I am older, a little wiser, and running out of time.

Years ago God showed me that I could be equally happy outside of track, outside of being a professional athlete. Over the last several years, I have enjoyed TV hosting and working in media. Through this I have discovered that I can have jobs that will challenge and fulfill me.

But I still have the burning question: What about that Olympic medal?

I still have time.

Yes, I'm older and a little bit more beat up, but I still have the capability to compete at a high level for a few more years. And I still have a desire to finish. So I am going to enjoy these next few years.

In 2019, I began working toward making the Olympic US hurdles team for 2020 in Japan. But COVID hit, and everything came to a standstill.

Then Kaillie Humphries, the two-time Olympic champion, three-time Olympic medalist, and reigning world champion, DMed (direct messaged) me on Instagram.

Kaillie had previously competed for Canada and is a friend. She had recently married an American and was competing for Team USA. She wanted me to come back to bobsledding.

It was a tough decision, because I'd gotten close to a medal the last go-round with bobsled. But then, after getting concussed and what felt like some inside politics, I had lost my spot for the 2018 Olympics. But Kaillie made it clear I would have a legit shot at making the team.

Okay, God, you know I'm running low on strength, but I'm not all the way out. And I'm ready to take another step, I prayed.

Kaillie was right. As of this writing I have not only made the bobsled team, but Kaillie and I have also won a world championship.

> On Friday and Saturday [February 5 and 6, 2021], Humphries piloted and Jones pushed the fastest two-woman bobsled in the world. They prevailed by .35 of a second over Germans Kim Kalicki and Ann-Christin Strack combining times from four runs in Altenberg, Germany.
>
> Jones, one of 10 U.S. athletes to compete in both a Summer and Winter Olympics, earned the most prestigious [world championship] title of her career on either type of track at age 38.[2]

This opens the door for a possible fourth Olympic berth in 2022.

Following the win, I spoke with reporters about a possible return to Beijing "where it all went wrong" and another opportunity to win a gold medal.

> What [has] always been very important [for me] is facing my fears. And in 2008, I was winning that race, and I hit a hurdle and it cost me Olympic gold. Nothing would mean more to me than to face my fears of [fourteen] years of being ridiculed for not getting an Olympic medal.[3]

Can I make it happen? I don't know. But we are in the home stretch. We're in the last part of this long, long race, and I'm going to do my hardest to return to Beijing. I would love for people to be encouraged by that persistence, determination, and all the cliché things that Olympians say.

You know how I feel about clichés? They are simply truths so powerful they bear repeating. Attack, attack, attack. Keep going. Don't quit. Work harder than everyone around you, then work even harder. Believe in yourself, forgive yourself, forgive those who hurt you along the way, practice gratitude, trust God, trust God, trust God.

Did I mention don't quit?

These truths aren't clichés to me.

And when it comes to an Olympic medal, after coming up short so many times, I am thankful for this opportunity to compete in Beijing and to show people I didn't quit, that I went all the way to the end, that whether I win or lose, I took a full lap around that track.

ACKNOWLEDGMENTS

To God, thank you—for it all. For the ups and the downs. For the hurdles we clear and for the ones we don't. Thank you for the wins and the losses.

To Coach Shaver: my athletic career has lasted so long with you, I don't know who will retire first.

To Coach Mike Kohn, head coach of USA Bobsled; Coach Ferguson, summer track/Junior Olympics; Coach Stu McMillan, 2014 Winter Olympics; and Coach Dick Hewins, my high school coach.

To my teammates Katie Uhlaender, Chaunté Howard Lowe, and Wallace Spearmon: if not for Beijing, we could've retired ages ago.

To Nia Ali: When you didn't make the Olympic team in 2012, you took time to congratulate me. I'm glad to see where God has taken you.

To Kaillie Humphries for the smooth rides.

To Alysia Montaño and Ilana Tub.

To Stephanie Durst, the best training partner I ever had: I wouldn't have made one Olympic team without you.

To Jazmine Fenlator: I wrote a whole nice chapter about you, so now you have to apologize for our last fight.

To Nick Cunningham, my interim bobsled coach.

To my agent Brandon Swibel: there is not a sentence that would do justice for how grateful I am to have you in my life.

To my agent Paul Doyle: thank you for fighting so hard for the athletes and the sport of track and field.

To the churches and people whose podcasts encouraged me: the Salvation Army and Healing Place Church; Charles Stanley and Robert Schuller.

To my foster parents, Randy Essex, Marilyn Hawk, and Janice and Ronnie Caldwell.

To Sichin Li-McCall, my neighbor who cooks for me when I'm injured.

To Lorenda Arceneaux for talks that encourage me to continue to wait for my husband.

To Wendy Winans, for keeping me spiritually strong when I felt weak.

To all the surgeons who have repaired me like rag doll Annie, including my spinal surgeon, Dr. Robert Bray; my hip surgeon, Dr Marc Philippon; and my shoulder surgeon, Dr. Andrew Bulczynski.

To athletic trainers around the world who are underpaid and overworked.

To my doctors: Dr. Myles Jaynes, Dr. Donald Carson, Dr. Byrne, and Dr. Mara.

To my chiropractors: Dr. Ripley from college and the 2008 and 2012 Olympics, Dr. Dustin Nabhan at the Olympic Training Center in Colorado Springs, Dr. Jon Wilhelm, Dr. Jon Hymel, Dr. John Ball, and Dr. James O'Toole.

To my acupuncturist: Bret Moldenhauer.

To the physical therapists who helped me rehab: Robby Bolton and Steve Levins.

To my massage therapists: Jill Neiubug and Brenner Corry. And to the thousand other massage therapists I have used while traveling who kneaded my muscles like pizza dough to get one more day out of my legs. Thank you.

To Tim Reynolds for his pep talks.

To David Velasquez—gorrrrrrrg!!!

To Adam Schmenk for keeping the camera on me when I cried at the Olympics. Thanks! I'm an ugly crier, and now everyone knows.

To the basketball coach in middle school who gave me rides to games, the middle school girl who loaned me a pair of shoes to run track meets in, and the science teacher who turned our water back on when it got cut off.

To Roosevelt High School.

To Des Moines, Iowa, for a great childhood.

To the Drake Relays for funnel cakes and my first big race that sparked it all.

To the Penn Relays for curry goat and Philly cheesecake.

To the American Track League for opportunities when there were none.

To the USATF, the IAAF/World Athletics, and the USA Bobsled.

To all the hurdlers I trained or ever ran against. Thank you for providing good rhythm and competition. We feed off each other.

To my family.

To Troy, James, and Charles.

To Angie and Chrissy.

To Aunt Mary, Aunt Annette, Aunt Jenny, and Aunt Stephanie.

To Mom and Dad: I turned out all right because of you guys.

To the rest of my family: There are really too many of y'all to name. But if your last name is Jones or Counter . . .

To Jason Clark: I squeezed you and a book came out.

ACKNOWLEDGMENTS

To Sarah Ward for the book cover.

To everyone at Nelson Books who edited this book: bless you for your hard work, because I don't even know if it's spelled *grammar* or *grammer*.

To Esther Fedorkevich and everyone at the Fedd Agency.

To all the guys who rejected me or ghosted me: my future husband thanks you.

And lastly, to all the people who have ever beaten me in a race: I used it as motivation. Thank you.

NOTES

Chapter 1: But You're Here

1. Sean Gregory, "Lolo's No Choke," *Time*, July 19, 2012, https://olympics.time.com/2012/07/19/lolo-jones-olympic-hurdler/.
2. Olivier Poirier-Leroy, "What Are My Chances of Going to the Olympics?" YourSwimBook, accessed March 3, 2021, https://www.yourswimlog.com/what-are-my-chances-of-going-to-the-olympics/.
3. Luke Parker, "Lolo Jones: Overcoming the Odds," *The Unbroken Mentality* podcast, May 4, 2020.
4. Parker, "Lolo Jones: Overcoming the Odds."

Chapter 2: Dad (My First Coach) and Forgiveness

1. "Lolo Jones—I'm Praying for Oscar Pistorius . . . My Dad Was a Killer Too," *TMZ Sports*, October 23, 2014, https://www.youtube.com/watch?v=42xNmxM0Mn4.
2. Christine Thomasos, "Lolo Jones Receives Backlash for Posing with Floyd Mayweather Jr. After Domestic Violence History; Track Athlete Says Her Father Was Former Abuser," *Christian Post*, May 4, 2015, https://www.christianpost.com/news/lolo-jones-receives-backlash-for-posing-with-floyd-mayweather-jr-after-domestic-violence-history-track-athlete-says-her-father-was-former-abuser.html.

3. Thomasos, "Lolo Jones Receives Backlash."

4. Thomasos, "Lolo Jones Receives Backlash."

Chapter 3: Mom, Poverty, and Learning to Work

1. "Programs: BOOK IT!," Pizza Hut, accessed March 13, 2021, https://www.bookitprogram.com/programs/book-it.

Chapter 5: A Biracial Girl in a Black and White World

1. Lolo Jones, Instagram post, June 13, 2020, https://www.instagram.com/p/CBZP-nWBRfJ/.

2. Yannick RIPA, "Women and the Olympic Games," EHNE (Digital Encyclopedia of European History), June 22, 2020, https://ehne.fr/en/encyclopedia/themes/gender-and-europe/gendered-body/women-and-olympic-games.

3. World Athletics, "100 Metre Hurdles," accessed April 9, 2021, https://worldathletics.org/disciplines/hurdles/100-metres-hurdles.

Chapter 6: Breakthrough

1. "Lolo Jones Punches 2008 Olympics Ticket with Thrilling 100m Run at Trials," NBC Sports, YouTube, posted August 12, 2020, https://www.youtube.com/watch?v=eC-gbZn-4A0.

2. 2012 income survey, USA Track and Field Foundation, cited in Kurt Badenhausen, "The Highest-Paid Athletes at the Rio Summer Olympics," *Forbes*, August 3, 2016, https://www.forbes.com/sites/kurtbadenhausen/2016/08/03/the-highest-paid-summer-olympic-athletes-at-rio/?sh=659d76d11584.

3. Rob Harris, "As Rio Relies on Free Labor, IOC Execs Get $900 per Diems," AP News, August 11, 2016, https://apnews.com/article/6cc782458d7746fc9eac4c71dbccd025.

4. "United States Olympic & Paralympic Committee Tax Disclosures (Form 990)," Finance, Team USA, accessed March 16, 2021, https://www.teamusa.org/footer/finance.

5. *The Weight of Gold*, directed by Brett Rapkin (New York: HBO, 2020).

6. Information in this section is drawn from Namita Nayyar, "Lolo Jones: Success Story Built on Foundation of Failures," *Women's Fitness*, September 10, 2013, https://www.womenfitness.net/loloJones _foundation.htm.

7. This is according to Paul Doyle, track and field agent. Also, when I ran the IAAF Golden League, the first-place prize money was $16,000. Now, it's $10,000.

Chapter 7: An Inspiration

1. Interview by Bob Neumeier, NBC, August 19, 2008, quoted in King Kaufman, "Lolo Jones' Olympian Failure," *Salon*, August 20, 2008, https://www.salon.com/2008/08/20/jones_4/.

2. Quoted in Liz Colville, "The Olympians: Lolo Jones," findingDulcinea, August 20, 2008, http://www.findingdulcinea.com/features/sports /olympians/Lolo-Jones.html.

3. Quoted in Nick Mulvenney, "Jones Crashes and Burns, Harper's Surprise," August 19, 2008, Reuters, https://www.reuters.com /article/us-olympics-athletics-women-hurdles-quot/jones-crashes -and-burns-harpers-surprise-idUSSP4505120080819.

4. Quoted in Lynn Zinser, "On the Track, a Cruel Loss and Surprising Victories," August 19, 2008, *New York Times*, https://www.nytimes .com/2008/08/20/sports/olympics/20track.html.

5. Interview by Matt Lauer, *Today*, NBC, August 20, 2008, https://www .youtube.com/watch?v=KsywkoNj8xI.

6. "Olympics '08: First Person with Lolo Jones," Associated Press, August 20, 2008, https://www.youtube.com/watch?v=XySvRYIh9Tg.

7. "Lolo Jones Talks of Disappointing Race," YouTube, October 30, 2008, https://www.youtube.com/watch?v=lfH-0keiTMg.

8. Coach Grant Taylor, *Facing the Giants*, directed by Alex Kendrick (n.p.: Carmel Entertainment Group, 2006).

9. "Lolo Jones Talks About God's Role in Sports and Her Haters," *First Take*, ESPN, February 1, 2013, https://www.youtube.com/watch?v =Da5yYw1TzDM.

Chapter 8: Waiting, Dating, and Trusting

1. "Lolo Jones Until Marriage," interview by Mary Carillo, *Real Sports with Bryant Gumbel*, episode 182, HBO Sports, May 21, 2012, https://www.youtube.com/watch?v=h_SRO9mpt4Y.

2. "Lolo Jones Talks Virginity," interview by Mary Carillo *Real Sports with Bryant Gumbel*, HBO Sports, March 2013, https://youtube.com/watch?v=x1Wpv6-6BHs.

3. "Lolo Jones Until Marriage."

4. "Lolo Jones Until Marriage."

5. Brandon Gaille, "45 Statistics on Cohabitation Before Marriage," *BrandonGaille* (blog), May 20, 2017, https://brandongaille.com/43-statistics-on-cohabitation-before-marriage/; Scott Stanley, "Premarital Cohabitation Is Still Associated with Greater Odds of Divorce," *Institute for Family Studies* (blog), October 17, 2018, https://ifstudies.org/blog/premarital-cohabitation-is-still-associated-with-greater-odds-of-divorce; and W. Bradford Wilcox, ed., *The State of Our Unions: Marriage in America 2009* (Charlottesville, VA: National Marriage Project, 2009), 75.

6. "Lolo Jones Until Marriage."

7. "Lolo Jones Until Marriage."

8. "Lolo Jones Until Marriage."

Chapter 9: Without Vision

1. Julia Savacool, "Lolo Jones Clears Latest Hurdle: Spine Surgery," ESPN, November 9, 2011, https://www.espn.com/espnw/journeys-victories/story/_/id/7213167/spine-surgery.

2. Savacool, "Lolo Jones Clears Latest Hurdle."

3. "Lolo Jones Back Micro Surgery," DISCmdgroup, YouTube, January 4, 2013, https://www.youtube.com/watch?v=YOu4L436Xew.

4. "Lolo Jones Back Micro Surgery."

5. "Lolo Jones—I'm Soooo Drugged Up . . . Keep Bill Cosby Away!" TMZ.com, accessed March 17, 2021, https://www.tmz.com/videos/0-892v98qb/.

6. "Lolo Jones Back Micro Surgery."

7. Savacool, "Lolo Jones Clears Latest Hurdle."

8. "Lolo Jones, Dawn Harper, Kellie Wells Your 110m Hurdle Olympic Team," LetsRun.com, YouTube, June 23, 2012, https://www.youtube .com/watch?v=lWT4yn9KlZU.

9. ASICS, "ASICS Athlete Lolo Jones Secures Her Spot to London," news release, June 23, 2012, https://assets.asics.com/page_types/1667/files /20120625_original.pdf?1386146166.

Chapter 10: The Inquisition of Lolo Jones

1. Tim Layden, "Jones Misses Glory in 100 Hurdles, While Manzano Wraps Historic 1,500," *Sports Illustrated*, August 7, 2012, https://www .si.com/more-sports/2012/08/08/womens-hurdles-mens-1500.

2. NBC interview, quoted in Christine Thomasos, "Lolo Jones 'Shocked' by Dawn Harper and Kellie Wells' Criticism," *Christian Post*, August 22, 2012, https://www.christianpost.com/news/lolo -jones-shocked-by-dawn-harper-and-kellie-wells-olympics-criticism .html.

3. Sean Gregory, "Lolo Jones Finishes Fourth in the Olympics. So Did She Deserve to Be Heard?" *Time*, August 7, 2012, https://olympics .time.com/2012/08/07/lolo-jones-finishes-fourth-in-the-olympics -so-did-she-deserve-to-be-heard/.

4. Jeré Longman, "For Lolo Jones, Everything Is Image," *New York Times*, August 4, 2012, https://www.nytimes.com/2012/08/05 /sports/olympics/olympian-lolo-jones-draws-attention-to-beauty -not-achievement.html.

5. Longman, "For Lolo Jones, Everything Is Image."

6. Janice Forsyth, quoted in Longman, "For Lolo Jones, Everything Is Image."

7. Dawn Harper interview by Michelle Beadle, 2012, quoted in Tony Manfred, "Two American Hurdlers Ripped Lolo Jones in an Awkward NBC Interview This Morning," *Business Insider*, August 8, 2012, https://www.businessinsider.com/harper-wells-lolo-jones -interview-2012-8.

8. "Lolo Jones on Rio Olympics, Comeback and Critics,"
   CBS This Morning, January 5, 2016, https://www.youtube.com
   /watch?v=XxX5hTEJkNE.
9. *Cool Runnings*, directed by John Turteltaub (Burbank, CA:
   Walt Disney Pictures, 1993), https://www.youtube.com
   /watch?v=tYRtTqx-IK8.

Chapter 11: Win or Lose, I'll Praise Him

1. *Encyclopaedia Britannica*, s.v. "Bobsledding," https://www.britannica
   .com/sports/bobsledding.
2. "Winter Olympics 2014: USBSF Defends Lolo Jones' Selection to
   Compete in Sochi," Associated Press, January 24, 2014, updated
   March 27, 2019, https://www.cleveland.com/olympics/2014/01
   /winter_olympics_2014_usbsf_def.html.

Afterword

1. "Lolo Jones Back in Bobsled, Seeking Elusive Olympic Medal and
   Return to Beijing," NBC Sports, November 27, 2020, https://olympics.
   nbcsports.com/2020/11/27/lolo-jones-bobsled-olympics/.
2. Nick Zaccardi, "Kaillie Humphries, Lolo Jones Win Historic Bobsled
   World Championship," NBC Sports, February 6, 2021, https://
   olympics.nbcsports.com/2021/02/06/kaillie-humphries-lolo-jones
   -bobsled-world-championship/.
3. "Lolo Jones Back in Bobsled."

ABOUT THE AUTHOR

Lolo Jones is a highly accomplished American athlete in hurdling and bobsledding, competing in three Olympics and securing the title of world champion four times. She is one of only ten American athletes in history to compete in both the Winter and Summer Olympics. She was favored to win the 100-meter hurdles at the 2008 Beijing Olympics, where she held the lead until hitting the penultimate hurdle and finished in seventh place. Lolo is currently training to compete in the 2022 Winter Olympic Games in pursuit of winning her first Olympic medal. Currently residing in Louisiana, she speaks openly about her Christian faith and is committed to empowering and inspiring those who face socioeconomic hardships through the Lolo Jones Foundation.